Asylum

Asylum

A Mid-Century Madhouse and Its Lessons about Our Mentally Ill Today

Enoch Callaway, M.D.

Westport, Connecticut
London

Library of Congress Cataloging-in-Publication Data

Callaway, Enoch.
  Asylum: a mid-century madhouse and its lessons about our mentally ill today /
  Enoch Callaway.
    p. cm.
  Includes bibliographical references and index.
  ISBN–13: 978–0–275–99704–5 (alk. paper)
  ISBN–10: 0–275–99704–9 (alk. paper)
1. Worcester State Hospital—History. 2. Psychiatric hospitals—Massachusetts—
Worcester—History. I. Title.
[DNLM: 1. Worcester State Hospital. 2. Hospitals, Psychiatric—history—Massachusetts.
3. History, 20th Century—Massachusetts. 4. Psychiatry—history—Massachusetts.
WM 28 AM4 W923C 2007]
RC445.M43W67 2007
362.2'1097443—dc22   2007014365

British Library Cataloguing in Publication Data is available.

Library of Congress Catalog Card Number: 2007014365
ISBN-13: 978–0–275–99704–5
ISBN-10: 0–275–99704–9

First published in 2007

Praeger Publishers, 88 Post Road West, Westport, CT 06881
An imprint of Greenwood Publishing Group, Inc.
www.praeger.com

Printed in the United States of America

The paper used in this book complies with the
Permanent Paper Standard issued by the National
Information Standards Organization (Z39.48-1984).

10 9 8 7 6 5 4 3 2 1

This book is dedicated to my two Dorothys,
In fond memory of the first, and with gratitude to the second.

Table of Contents

Foreword   xi

Acknowledgments   xiii

Introduction   xv

Part One: In The Home For Broken Minds   1

1   Welcome to the Lunatic Asylum   3

2   Back Wards   7

3   Isn't That Depressing?   10

4   Promotion To Jesus   13

5   Doctor Charisma   17

6   Are You There?   20

7   Insulin Coma (aka Insulin Shock) Therapy   22

8   By These Signs Shall Ye Know Them   26

9   Electroconvulsive Therapy (ECT)   28

10   The Last Resort   31

11   Beauty Is As Beauty Does   33

12   Some Comments on the Subject of Schizophrenia   36

13   We May Be Crazy But We're Not Stupid   40

14   My Exhibitionism Gets a Lucky Break   42

15	Truth Serum	44
16	The Pet Paranoid	47
17	The Patient Who Smelled Like a Darkroom	50
18	Psychiatry, The Cinderella Of Medicine, before the Fairy Godmother (aka the Pharmaceutical Industry) Discovered Glass Slippers for Her Feet	53
19	Never Say Die	56
20	Folie À Deux	59
21	My Nose Receives a Silver Rod at Harvard	61
Part Two: Doctor, Please Make The Voices Go Away		**65**
22	A Special Place.	67
23	The Moon and Madness	71
24	Electronic Relics of the Pre-Penicillin Era	73
25	Hydrotherapy	75
26	The Psychoanalytic Citation	78
27	A Saint for the Schizophrenics	80
28	Deafness and Despair	83
29	Coarse Brain Damage	85
30	Psychosomatic Medicine	87
31	The Magic Mirror	89
32	The Dark Side	91
33	Behind the Wall of Silence	94
34	Gather Ye Labwear Where Ye May	97
35	Miscellaneous Misadventures	101
36	The Fortunate Failure	103
37	He Who Calls His Neighbor a Fool	108
38	The Genital Sentinel	111
39	Did She Die from Counter-Transference?	114

Part Three: Leaders Of The Vision   119

40   Fabulous Phonies   121

41   The Psychoanalytic Innovator   125

42   How Fortune Came to Favor the Foundation and the Hospital   129

43   From Madhouse to Mansion   135

44   On Mink Mating and Money-Making   137

45   Nate Kline   139

46   Marvelous Mentors   141

47   Consensual Validation: The Movie *Snake Pit*   146

48   Footnotes on Psychotherapy   149

Part Four: It's Only The Castle Burning   155

49   Welcome to the Third Millenium   157

50   Visits With Those Left Behind   161

51   Are Promises Made To Be Broken?   166

52   The Seeds of Deinstitutionalization   170

53   The Unholy Aliance   177

54   Postscript: So What? With Notes on the Culture of Caring   183

Appendix   189

Notes   191

Index   195

Foreword

I first met Dr. "Noch" Callaway in 1976, when I had just finished my residency and had been appointed as a clinical instructor at the University of California San Francisco in the department of psychiatry. Dr. Callaway was known to junior faculty members, such as me, as an outstanding clinician, psychopharmacologist, and researcher. When any of us had a patient with severe mental illness who was not responding to our treatments, we would get a consultation from Dr. Callaway about how we might combine several treatments or think of a novel regimen.

Dr. Callaway has written an illuminating book that details what psychiatric practice entailed in the late 1940s. He describes his professional and personal journey as a psychiatrist at Worcester State Hospital and gives a history of psychiatric treatments that were available then. Before the modern era of psychopharmacology, there was insulin shock therapy, ECT, and even lobotomies. Dr. Callaway describes these treatments in a manner that makes us feel as if we were with him, watching patients being treated. His description reminds us of the tremendous advances of psychopharmacology and other available treatments for patients with severe mental illness. He describes the era of long term hospitalizations that existed before the community mental health era, and the era of managed care oversight that has led to brief hospitalizations.

In the twenty-first century, we have a much larger armamentarium of treatments. Dr. Callaway's book reminds us of how far psychiatry has come. His insights and descriptions make a valuable historical contribution to the education of all clinicians who work with patients who have severe mental illness, and will be of great interest to the general public as well. Family members of severely mentally ill patients will find this book helpful in their appreciation of treatment available now. In addition, medical students and residents will benefit from learning about the change in trends in psychiatric treatment.

Now I better understand the long journey that Dr. Callaway underwent that led to his eminence as a premiere consultant and educator.

Renee Binder, M.D.
Prof of Psychiatry, University of California at San Francisco
Past Pres. California Psychiatric Assn.

Acknowledgments

Thanks to Lou and Tom Mongan, Alan Gevins, and Aubrey Metcalf for early encouragement. Then there was the creator of wisecracking, crime-busting Amanda Pepper, Gillian Roberts, who in her everyday role of Judy Greber, the best of all neighbors, was so honest in her appraisal of my first attempt to write a novel that since then I have concentrated on these memoirs. Credit must also go to Dr. Sarah Brabant, my sister. Emily Leider, poet turned biographer (Gertrude Atherton, May West, and Rudolph Valentino), offered encouragement. She is, not incidentally, the daughter of Joe Wortis, the psychiatrist whom I describe in the book as my long time role model. Then there were paid editors and readers who served me well, including Dr. Hitzig and Shirley Singer.

There are also writers whose works have informed my opinions, but could not be comfortably cited in the text. They are Drivery and Bernardet,[1] Diekman,[2] Goldman et al,[3] Grob,[4] Jamison,[5] and Linehan.[6] Their works are cited only in the notes.

Finally, I thank Angela Browne-Miller, my editor, who deserves a healthy share of credit for any literary virtues this work may have. Thus said, I feel it only fair for me to indulge in a post-penultimate relâchement of my propensity for pompous polysyllabic phraseology of exotic provenance. As the apotheosis of Strunkian[7] simplicity, I have duly worshiped her admonishments, but as for this final fling, further criticism of my prolixity is something up with which I will not put.

Introduction

In the interval between WW II and the Korean conflict, about 3,000 mental patients lived in a baroque castle-like hospital on a 500 acre farm on the outskirts of Worcester, Massachusetts. Living in that same building were research scientists, clinical staff (social workers, nurses, occupational therapists, etc.), and about a dozen young "resident physicians" (psychiatrists in training). Such trainees are still referred to as "residents," although today they rarely reside in their hospitals as we did. We had been rushed through college and medical school to meet wartime needs, but had never seen combat. We were thus younger and more naïve than usual, with all the expected good and bad qualities associated with youth.

An almost blind faith in psychoanalysis was at its high water mark. Those of us who were true believers "knew" that a sufficiently deep analysis would cure any mental illness. Even among those who dared to question the therapeutic claims made by the psychoanalysts, most still saw the world as entirely rational and logical. We believed in a universe tightly ordered by discoverable laws, and so we searched for grand theories that would link psychology, mathematics, and biology.

In 1833, the first state hospital for the mentally ill was founded as the Worcester Insane Asylum. In those days, mental hospitals were referred to as "asylums." That was quite an appropriate term. It is derived from the Latin word "sylo," which means "the right of seizure." With the ablative "A," it means "no right of seizure," or a place where one is protected from arrest. In general, the asylums did protect patients from the criminal justice system. Lack of such protection is one of the shortcomings of today's system, even with all the dramatic advances in treatment over the past century.

Worcester State Hospital always had its ups and downs, but J.P. Morrisy[1] called his book about it *The Enduring Asylum*. However, nothing endures, and between 1950 and 1995, this asylum went from an outstanding center for psychiatric teaching, research, and clinical practice to a charred hulk. Its immolation epitomized the end of an era, and there are only a few of us left who remember those earlier times. Since then, the advances in care for the mentally ill have surpassed the wildest dreams that we had in the beginning. Not only has psychopharmacology revolutionized the field, but evidence-based practices in psychotherapy and community mental health are available. We are also confident that new miracles in brain imaging and genetics are waiting in the wings. Nonetheless, a significant portion of the mentally ill remains underserved. Perhaps these anecdotes from that forgotten world will add a new perspective to dilemmas of freedom and asylum we face.

Part I

IN THE HOME FOR BROKEN MINDS

I

Welcome to the Lunatic Asylum

Imagine if you will a 500-acre working farm extending from the lip of a high bluff down to a valley and a broad road. It is 1948, and this road is the old Worcester-Boston highway, supplanted now by the new freeway. Where the farm abuts that road, a formidable stone wall with a great iron gate stands guard, although the gate is never closed. As we go through the open gate, we find ourselves in an extensive and inviting park with manicured grounds. The road meanders among stately old trees and giant rhododendrons, past neat cottages for senior staff, and then passes through the porte-cochère of the forbidding buildings of the Worcester State Hospital.

Even in 1948, this is a baroque architectural anachronism, out of place in the tidy New England countryside. It is constructed of formidable four-foot-square reddish stones, and one can not help noticing the barred windows and heavily screened sun-porches. It is obviously a fortress defending the mentally ill inmates from society. At the same time it is their prison. The young residents who come here to be trained will see repeatedly how psychological fortresses, like asylums, become prisons. Hopefully, they will learn how safety is often incompatible with love and the other great adventures of a full life.

The porte-cochère is attached to a grand stairway, which leads up to the central administration building's entrance. That in turn is topped by a baroque bell tower which extends another story above the three-story building proper. Flanking the administration building on both its sides are the two clinical wings; female on the left and male on the right. They are built back from the administration building in a series of offsets designed to bring sunlight onto all the sun-porches. The result is a labyrinth of walkways and courtyards, perhaps unintentionally imitating the labyrinth we call the human mind. It is easy to imagine one of Charles Addam's spooky cartoon characters peeking from the bell tower. There was a local newspaper writer who saw in this place the suggestion of a

WORCESTER LUNATIC HOSPITAL, BLOOMINGDALE.

Three views of Worcester State Hospital. A. From the ground around 1885, B. From the air around 1968. C. Details of a building.

All pictures courtesy of the Worcester Historical Museum, Worcester Mass.

"cozy" medieval city, but I think he must have been descended from Pollyanna.

The design of the building is not without logic. Each of the two clinical wings extending from either side of the central Administration Building has three sub-wings, with each sub-wing set back from its neighbor. The more ready for discharge, the closer to the front a patient is housed, and the more chronic, the higher up he or she is housed. Since being both chronically mentally ill and being ready for discharge are generally incompatible, the third floors of each sub-wing nearest the front are for the medically and surgically ill. This is a complete hospital within a hospital. There is a staff surgeon and a staff internist. There are X-ray facilities and an operating suite for both emergency surgery and for elective surgery, all serving patients too disturbed for transfer to the general hospital in the town proper, the city of Worcester.

Off to the right and behind the hospital are the laundry, the dairy, and the farm. They supply food and clean linens to the hospital and industrial therapy for the patients. Finally, five miles away, near the center of Worcester and fronting on Summer Street, stands the original old hospital, built in 1833. This ancient building serves as an overflow warehouse for chronic patients that seem beyond salvation.

In these years of the late 40s and early 50s, there are about 3,000 patients and maybe 1,000 employees, but only about 30 of them are physicians. The ratio of nurses and attendants to patients is about one to twenty, which means on average a single nurse or attendant must care for 100 patients at night. That will change in the next 50 years, partly because of legislation and partly because of actions by state employees' unions. For example, by the year 2000, California law will require one staff member for eight patients in the day and one for sixteen patients at night. Big changes lay ahead, and, of course, not just in patient/staff ratios.

The hospital we are visiting in the 1940s has food of such poor quality that, in the winter, back wards patients who can not go outside to supplement their diets verge on having clinical scurvy, at least according to the low levels of vitamin C found in their blood. The back wards and basement corridors smell of excrement and disinfectant. Iron rings are imbedded in the walls of basement corridors, and it is rumored that these rings had been used to restrain patients in the "early days." But Worcester pioneered the treatment of mental patients without restraints as early as 1900, and so, in 1948, Worcester rarely uses restraint of any sort. Needless to say, patients are never chained to basement walls.

As I arrive at Worcester in those years before the Psychopharmacological Revolution, the selection of drugs for treating mental illness is, by modern standards, laughably inadequate. The first paper introducing chlorpromazine for the treatment of schizophrenia will not be published until 1952. So the doctors make do with shock treatments and barbiturate sedatives, while laboring with unbounded, and equally unfounded, faith in the psychoanalytic approach to treating psychotics. Meanwhile, warehouse-like rooms fill with deteriorated patients who have defeated our best efforts. In short, the Worcester State Hospital I have asked you to imagine with me is both a snake pit and a model mental hospital circa 1950. For some of the mentally ill, this is a safe house where they can recover, but for too many others it is a terminal warehouse. Please keep this strange picture in mind as I tell you my memories of that past.

When I entered Worcester to begin my psychiatric residency in 1948, my first two contacts were with the superintendent, Dr. Flower, and the clinical director, Dr. Rothschild. Bardwell Flower, MD, was the grand high lord of the Worcester State Hospital's considerable fiefdom. He was a man of ample proportions with an amiable disposition. Since he was a Harvard Medical School graduate he probably had a better than average education. However, when speaking before a group, his style was so in keeping with his baroque institution that it was comic. I joined a group of first year residents consisting of seven men and one woman. For our welcoming talk, Dr. Flower began, "Lady and gentlemen, I disremember whether these brochures were sent to you in advance. In any event I possess additional copies of which you may avail yourselves for perusal at your leisure." The house staff affectionately referred to him as Fartwell Blower.

Second in command was the clinical director, Dr. David Rothschild. Where Flower was ample and verbose, Rothschild was spare in both frame and speech. He was a bachelor who had a suite of rooms in the hospital, and his life revolved around his enormous clinical responsibility. He was a dedicated and gifted clinician, who year after year had to deal with young doctors as immature and over-enthusiastic as we were. He was always tactful, but somehow we knew not to argue with him. Among the residents, it was said that when you wanted to ask Dr. Rothschild for something, you should wait until he had his hands out of the pockets of his white coat. When he had his hands in his pockets, he always said "No!"

The professional staff I joined included physicians, nurses, psychologists, occupational therapists, social workers, and research scientists from the Worcester Foundation for Experimental Biology. All the residents were from first-rate medical schools and internships. There were several physician-couples, although female MD's were not all that common in those days. Many of the other wives were trained professionals who joined their husbands by working in the hospital as nurses, occupational therapists, etc. For all that the setting was bizarre, the food lousy, and the conditions shocking at first, our heterogeneous group lived and worked together in enforced isolation with amazing enthusiasm and good humor. In a sense, we were all inmates at Worcester.

I have not seen a case in over 40 years. We also have not had an encephalitis epidemic in about 90 years, so the post-encephalitic Parkinson's disease patients are all dead by now. By themselves, these two changes in medical epidemiology helped depopulate the back wards.

In today's homes for the elderly, demented patients now sit nodding quietly in chairs, thanks to minor tranquilizers such as Valium (diazepam), antipsychotics like Haldol (haloperidol), and atypical antipsychotics like Seroquel (quietapine). Only the really tough cases end up on geropsychiatric units. Thus has modern psychopharmacology helped empty the back wards. On the not-so-positive side, there are still some really sick mental patients who could profit from custodial care (leaving aside the thorny issue of involuntary medication). Some lucky ones among these chronically mentally ill people are in prisons, or in heavily staffed diversion programs. The most unfortunate ones have been turned out on the streets, where they suffer from "recreational" drugs, physical abuse, neglect, and starvation.

Psychiatric back wards furnished part of the toughening or hardening process applied to medical students in those times, so we residents had already seen back wards. I had attended chronic disease clinics at Bellevue Hospital and Welfare Island in New York, and my fellow residents had been similarly desensitized to shocking conditions. I doubt if my training had left me with the ability to imagine how the back wards affected the un-calloused observer. However, my wife, with her Bachelor of Fine Arts degree, made it clear to me that her encounter with the back wards was the most distressing experience of her life.

The female wards were the worst. To begin with, the women were more difficult to manage. More often than not, a combative man could be subdued by a show of overwhelming force. But no matter how large a staff one assembled, often you could not intimidate an equally disturbed woman. She would fling herself on the group, biting and scratching at random.

In addition, the sight of disorganized and unkempt women was more distressing than the sight of back ward men. Perhaps it was because drunken men could be seen on the streets looking pretty disheveled, while, in those years, we were not accustomed to the "bag ladies" that one sees on our streets today.

The uniform of the back ward female patient was the "strong dress." I never knew whether it was named for a Mr. or Ms. Strong, or whether it was simply a descriptive adjective. The garment was made of heavy blue-gray canvas with reinforcements at the hems, sleeves, and v-neck. It went on over the head, and there were no belts or ties.

During the day, the patients were kept on sun-porches with tile floors and drains, so that their excrement could be hosed down. Their strong dresses were changed daily. The hospital had a beauty shop, but these

2

Back Wards

The second and third floors of the third wing back, on both male and female sides, contained the bizarre worlds referred to as the "back wards." There we warehoused our treatment failures. Here were the unfortunate people who had not responded either to the passage of time or to our best therapeutic efforts. They could now look forward to spending the rest of their lives receiving custodial care. Patients stood or sat, some responding to hallucinatory voices, some sunk in the deepest of depressions. Patients such as these, who suffer recurrent untreated psychotic episodes, whether schizophrenic or manic-depressive, often deteriorate. Their brain volumes actually become reduced and their delusions become impoverished and colorless. Thus they become more mentally retarded than mad.

In those days, these back wards were made even more dramatic by the movement disorder patients who were progressing through terminal dementia. There were rigid trembling Parkinsonians, writhing patients with Huntington's disease, "wing beating" Wilson's disease patients, and tertiary syphilitics with their foot-slapping walks.

The active research and teaching programs made Worcester State Hospital a wonderful, if awesome, place for a beginning psychiatrist. With the huge patient population, some individuals were always progressing from acute and active treatment to chronic custodial care. The irony was that the treatment failures, which ended up as chronic custodial cases on the back wards, furnished worst-case natural histories of mental illnesses that were invaluable for teaching. In addition, these back wards were stockrooms of subjects for research projects of all sorts.

Now, the grotesque back wards of the past no longer exist in this country. There are a variety of reasons, some good and some not so good, for their disappearance. On the positive side we have better staff/patient ratios, we have the newer psychoactive drugs, and there have been many advances in general medicine. For example, with the discovery of penicillin, central nervous system syphilis (dementia paralytica) disappeared.

3

Isn't That Depressing?

We young residents at Worcester did have personal lives apart from our dealings with patients, but our personal lives could not escape being influenced by our work. On top of that, most of the residents' wives were professionals who worked in the hospital, so when we first arrived, I thought it would be a good idea if my wife, Dorothy, could join the community more fully by taking a job as an attendant. The fact that I would let her try working as an attendant says something about my immaturity, something about my view of Dorothy as some sort of superwoman, and something about what medical school did to extinguish sensitivity.

I grew up in LaGrange, Georgia. That was a town of about 20,000 souls located in the west-central part of the state. It was somewhat limited culturally, to say the least. Just after I turned 17, I left to attend Columbia College in New York on a scholarship. I had been at college for about four months when World War II started, and from then on the academic demands of pre-medical classes and medical school were intense and continuous. So by the time I was a medical student at Columbia College of Physicians and Surgeons, I was intellectually over-trained and emotionally underdeveloped.

During my third year of medical school, I began courting an exceptional young lady. What with the shortage of available men towards the end of the war, I was accustomed to finding that I attracted women who would have ordinarily been out of my league, but she was a standout among my exceptional female acquaintances. Both her parents were published authors, she had lived in France, and now lived with three other professional artists in a fourth floor walkup on Beekman Place. She was a good cook, dancer and skier. She seemed the sort of Bohemian free-spirited superwoman who could master anything without half trying. So it never occurred to me that she would not find working with disturbed mental patients as challenging and exciting as I did.

That Dorothy gave it a game try suggests that she herself bought into the superwoman idea. But shortly after beginning to work as an women were too disorganized to cooperate. Thus, their hair was cut shoulder-length for hygienic reasons, and their straggly, unkempt tresses made the witches from Macbeth look chic. Since we had no effective and safe sedatives or tranquilizers, most of them milled about in aimless agitation, defecating and urinating as the urges arose.

In addition to the movement disorders (Huntington's, Parkinson's, and Wilson's diseases) and the dementias (schizophrenia or *dementia praecox*, syphilitic *dementia paralytica*, and post-encephalitic dementia) mentioned above, there were cases of Alzheimer's dementia, Pick's dementia, multi-infarct dementia, post-alcoholic dementia, post-brain trauma dementia, deterioration due to uncontrollable epilepsy. There were also a collection of very rare disorders (e.g., *tuberosclerosis*, a congenital disease characterized by dementia, epilepsy, and characteristic skin lesions), which we referred to as *fascinomata*.

Attention to hygiene was about all we had to offer our back ward patients. The syphilitics had gotten as much benefit as they could from penicillin and fever therapy, the Parkinsonians got scopolamine, which reduced their stiffness a bit while making their dementia worse, and we did what we could to treat the cardiovascular diseases. Most of the patients had ceased to recognize their visitors, so in most cases the visitors had ceased to visit.

There were always more women than men on the back wards. That, I am sure, reflected the tendency of women to live longer than men. They were also probably in better physical health than some older women in the outside community whose more intact minds allowed them to get by alone and without adequate health care. Our patients were kept as clean as feasible, fed regularly, exercised when possible, and checked for signs of physical diseases. Being just out of medical internships, the residents were always happy to show off their clinical skills in general medicine to the nursing staff. But, when I was called to do an annual review on one of those pathetic women, I could not help imagining her as a young woman, full of hope for the future, and never dreaming that she would end her days waiting for death in a warehouse full of broken minds.

attendant, she found herself trapped on a back ward staircase as demented women in strong dresses filed past on their way to a meal. Armed only with a ring of keys and a white cap, she was backed into a corner while the pathetic disheveled patients plucked and tugged at her uniform as they straggled past.

On the spot, Dorothy decided that work in a state mental hospital was not for her. She honored my devotion and enthusiasm for working with psychotic patients, but resigned her job as attendant and got herself a job as a substitute teacher in the local elementary school system. During my first year at Worcester State, we lived above a furniture store in Shrewsbury. So, while I worked at the state hospital, Dorothy made friends with the Shrewsbury townspeople and taught in local grade schools.

Shrewsbury was a charming New England village with a grassy commons at its center. On one side of the commons were the town buildings housing fire and police departments. On another side was a picture postcard Congregational church with a white steeple. Our furniture store was one of several businesses that also fronted on the commons.

The Worcester Foundation for Experimental Biology was actually in Shrewsbury, not Worcester. A number of their scientists lived in Shrewsbury. For example, among our neighbors above the furniture store was an Oriental couple, the Drs. Chang, who worked at the Foundation. The husband was later to gain fame as the chemist who, with Pincus, discovered the birth control pill. Mabel Jacobson was the wife of Dr. Jacobson, another foundation biochemist who played a pivotal role in developing the contraceptive pill. She and Dorothy became fast friends. They often met in the late afternoon to share some Old Mr. Boston, which was the cheapest sherry available.

Dorothy also became quite popular with other locals. Once, she forgot her keys to our apartment over the furniture store. Hearing of her predicament, the firemen came over from the fire department that was across the town square and gallantly used the hook and ladder to put one of their men through the apartment window so he could open the door for her.

Dorothy made friends with a young matron named Sally who also worked as a substitute teacher, and they car-pooled together when they both had assignments at the same school. One afternoon on the way home from teaching, Sally began to talk about her plans for the future. It turned out that her husband was trained as an undertaker and wanted to get a foothold as a funeral director in the Worcester area. Sally explained how hard it was to get into one of the established firms, and how impossible it was to start a new company.

Sally continued describing the steps her husband was taking and concluded by explaining how he was now doing freelance embalming, both to make a little money and also to get known by the local funeral parlors. Finally, she realized that she had been doing all the talking and so she asked Dorothy what her husband did.

"Oh, he's a psychiatrist at the state hospital," Dorothy said.

Sally looked horrified. "My God!" she exclaimed, "Isn't that depressing?"

Dorothy told that story to our fellow staff members and spouses, who had some good laughs at the idea of a freelance embalmer's wife thinking our profession was depressing. In retrospect, I suspect that Dorothy shared Sally's notion of what it was like to be a state hospital psychiatrist more than she let on. The living dead and the living mad are really more intimidating than are the dead dead.

Now, as I look back on my days at Worcester State, I wonder at the enthusiasm I shared with my fellow residents. I know I absolutely loved my work, despite the grim surroundings, the skimpy pay, and the lack of reinforcement that our fantasies of healing the mentally ill received. Perhaps it was the dehumanizing ways of medical schools in the 1940s that shaped our minds. We were introduced to cadavers on the first day or so, and about the same time told that a third of the freshman class would fail. Those who could not disassociate themselves from their feelings and develop some sort of insulation from reality left for other careers. I like to think those of us at Worcester were a compassionate group of physicians stimulated by the challenges of our field, but to the layman we must have seemed something of an oddly unfeeling bunch.

These reminiscences lead naturally to some observations about the tough-tender paradox that confronts all health care workers. It is obviously inappropriate and counterproductive for a therapist to turn away in disgust from a patient who confesses to some hidden horror. The surgeon must learn to overcome the normal aversion to cutting people, and the good nurse should learn not to make patients feel ashamed about involuntarily soiling themselves when she cleans up the mess. Physicians should be both fascinated and unoffended by pathology while still retaining compassion for the human suffering that results from that pathology. So if I am herein revealed as at least a little strange, I hope my compassion is answered by compassion in return.

4

Promotion to Jesus

Knowing so little and having virtually no effective pharmacological tools, it is amazing that we still managed to help people. Small unpredictable rewards are remarkably effective in maintaining behavior, and perhaps, like Skinner's rats, those random reinforcements played a role in our devotion to our work. At any rate, on those days, the simple virtues of respectful concern and calm competence could be seen unclouded by the powerful chemicals psychiatrists have come to rely on these days. The case of a patient I will call Sam Fuller (not his real name of course) illustrates the point.

I met Sam on a crisp fall evening. I had night duty on the male wings and so, after supper, I was catching up on some charts when Miss Gurrey at the switchboard rang my office. I understood how Miss Gurrey knew everything the staff talked about on the phone. She eavesdropped on all our calls. But I never figured out how she knew where everyone was all the time. Was she psychic or hyperaware? She had blond bangs with tiny curls, and since the musical *Oklahoma!!* was popular at the time, she was naturally known among the residents as "Gurrey with the fringe on top."

When I picked up the phone, she said, "Noch, the state troopers are bringing one in at this very moment. Mary'll pick you up on her way to admissions."

Mary was another story in herself. Mrs. Mary O'Reilley was the night nursing supervisor for the male side. She was some sort of a hybrid between the Earth Mother and a Sherman tank. So, with Mary at my side, I, weighing 160 pounds dripping wet and being quite devoted to my own safety, was quite unconcerned about taking a floridly psychotic patient off the hands of the state troopers.

Mary came by my office, and I followed her to the side door where the male admissions came in. Taking the big outdoor key, she opened the metal-clad door and welcomed the two husky state policemen and their prisoner into the asylum. The troopers flanked a black man of about 6'3'' who was in handcuffs and leg-irons. He was rail thin with a stubble beard and was dressed in threadbare overalls that were most inadequate for the weather at the time. He emitted an odor that, even over the background emanations from a body long unwashed, was nevertheless easily identified as one of chronic schizophrenia's classic signs. That smell has a sickly sweet quality and is not at all like the smell of stale healthy sweat, which, for example, one finds in sports locker rooms. The crushed leaves of the fetid iris give the closest match that I know. I cannot find the reference now, but I remember that around 1952 some research workers sterilized the skin of schizophrenics and normals, then collected sterile sweat by exercising them in plastic suits. The collected sweat showed that the schizophrenic sweat contained a smelly compound that normal sweat did not have.

One of the troopers said, "He was out on the turnpike directing traffic. Says he's God's police chief on earth."

The combination patient-prisoner pulled himself up into a commanding posture. With a regal voice he announced, "And that's the Lord's truth!"

The trooper gave him a contemptuous look and I for a moment I wondered if he was going to charge his prisoner with impersonating an officer. However, Mary spoke up. "OK boys, take the chains off. You can take them with you and call it a night."

The younger of the officers looked dubious but the older one had dealt with Mary before and reassured him, "They'll be all right." Turning to Mary, he said, "The papers are at the switchboard." Then the officers unshackled their ward, wished us good night, and departed. In that moment, prisoner became patient. I probably took the miraculous transformation for granted since I was relatively new to the strange world of the state hospital, and was so busy learning that nothing really struck me as odd.

Mary turned to our new patient and said, "What's your name?"

"Sam Turner, ma'am," he answered politely.

"When did you eat last, Sam?"

"I'm not sure."

"Well, Sam, let's go back where we can get you a bath. Then after the doctor examines you, we'll get you some food."

"Thank you, ma'am!"

The three of us marched back through the two front wards to the rearmost one where the most psychotic patients were housed. Then Mary left to go about her duties. The ward attendant led Sam to the shower while I opened the examining room and began putting together a chart. Soon Sam was delivered to me, dressed in a hospital bathrobe and smelling only of strong antiseptic soap.

I examined him and could not find anything wrong physically other than malnutrition, scratches, and insect bites. I could not get him to tell me anything about his family, and so I listened to his rambling account of how God spoke to him and how he advised God on improving the situation here on Earth. I was finishing my admission note when Sam's food arrived, so I turned him over to the attendant. Then I went back to my office, finished my charts, retired to bed in the residents' night duty room, and slept soundly as usual.

Sam settled into the routine of the acute back ward. I chatted with him briefly every day in hopes of getting some more usable history, and finally came to the conclusion that he had neither family nor any other social support system. Then, one day, Sam told me with great enthusiasm that God had just promoted him from Police Chief to Jesus. He elaborated on this in his usual disorganized way. Sam was both vague and repetitive, but as near as I could make out, Sam said God was pleased with his work as Police Chief and pretty disappointed with everyone else in the World.

One of the Occupational Therapy ladies told me that Sam had requested some yarn and a wooden hooking needle, and the next time I saw Sam he had embroidered the word *Jesus* on the back of his bathrobe. Meanwhile he seemed to be putting on a little weight, becoming more physically active, and also more actively psychotic. For example, at times he appeared to be actively hallucinating and conversing out loud with the hallucinations

One day we admitted a court case. An accused murderer had pled insanity and the court had committed him to the hospital for evaluation. Of course he too had to be put on the acute, back, first floor, maximum-security ward.

According to the attendant, it was nearly midnight when Sam's pacing and muttering to himself finally was more than the accused murderer could stand.

"Jesus Christ!" he exclaimed. "Quiet down so I can get some sleep."

With sonorous and pompous tones reminiscent of a Baptist minister, Sam replied, "Since you address me by my proper name, I will!" And he did.

Next morning, the accused man asked if he could please be returned to jail, explaining, "There's really crazy people in here and they scare me."

Shortly thereafter, I presented Sam to Dr. Rothschild at rounds. Rothschild commented that the acute back ward was probably just too stimulating for Sam, and recommended that I transfer him to a quieter chronic ward. Rothschild also suggested that I see about getting Sam into industrial therapy on the state hospital farm. Sam was certainly looking more and more agitated, and as usual I took the chief's advice.

After Sam went to work on the farm I no longer had regular contact with him, and was so busy that I did not think much about him until about a month later when the staff did their regular review of his case. Sam looked like a different person, for now he was 20 pounds heavier, shaved, and wearing pressed overalls with a clean blue shirt. I reviewed his history. Then Mr. Interbitzen, the industrial therapist in charge of the dairy, gave his report. He was a large, taciturn Norseman, who spoke with a faint lilting accent on the rare occasions when he made one of his laconic pronouncements. Interbitzen reported, "Sam's doin' well. Gets on good with the cows." Sam was sitting there listening and looking very pleased with himself until Mr. Interbitzen concluded, "We'll miss Sam if you discharge him."

Sam's face fell and his eyes got as large as saucers. Then he looked at Dr. Rothschild and said, "You can't discharge me. I'm crazy. I think I'm Jesus Christ!"

Rothschild replied, "Sam, we will not discharge you until you have some place to go that's better than this hospital. Now you go along with Mr. Interbitzen and don't you worry."

Years later, and after antipsychotics were in common use, elegant research showed that "low expressed emotionality" around schizophrenics increased the duration of their remissions and reduced the probability of their readmission. In other words, patients do not do well in families that get upset about delusions and hallucinations, and do better in families that seem more resigned to the symptoms of the schizophrenic. At Worcester, everyone recognized that Mr. Interbitzen and his cows were natural therapists for schizophrenics. Looking back on the therapeutic farm, I suspect that Interbitzen and his dairy cows were the ultimate in low expressed emotional responsiveness to psychotic behavior. I do not know what you could say to a cow to upset her.

Sad to say, such facilities no longer exist, since almost all state hospital farming operations were shut down years ago. That was due in part to the activity of the misguided do-gooders that feared that the farms were exploiting mental patients as involuntary peons. I have often wondered if the right wing defenders of agribusiness profits also played a supporting role in shutting down the state hospital farms, so that their constituents could make more money by supplying food to the hospitals, but how would one know?

Many years later, I had the opportunity to ask the head of psychiatry at the woman's prison in Chowchilla, California, whether they had ever considered giving prisoners pet animals as cheaper and safer tranquilizers than the drugs they used. She told me that they had indeed used "pet therapy" and it had been very successful, until a prisoner had been bitten and sued the state.

5

Doctor Charisma

While many of our patients were fascinating, some of the staff had them beat hands down. Dr. Hudson Hoagland, the co-director of the Worcester Foundation for Experimental Biology, was a shining example of the above. The complex interrelationships of the Worcester State Hospital and the Worcester Foundation for Experimental Biology will be described later (in Chapters 43 and 44). Here, the important fact is that when he gave the first year residents their introductory lectures on neurophysiology, he changed the course of my life, for better or worse. Because of Hoagland's charisma, he became my earliest scientific role model. He literally seduced me away from neuroendocrinology and into electroencephalography (brain electrical activity) with its fancy new EEG machines.

I must confess that my fascination with the electroencephalography was over-determined. As a boy, I used to hang out with a local ham (amateur) radio operator. Odd, but I still remember his call: W4KR. I longed to learn more about electronics. While my father would never have forbidden me to pursue any reasonable interest, he made it clear that he thought electronics was a waste of time for a future surgeon. When, many years later, Hoagland gave me permission to act on my enduring love affair with electronics, I was overjoyed.

Some decades later years, I have had cause to reconsidered my father's words of caution. Even when the digital computers of the 1980s let us record electrical potentials evoked from the brain by psychologically significant events, our dreamed-of electrophysiological "window on the mind" still seemed more like "a peep-hole into a hall of mirrors." Yet, while all the promises of insights in to mental illness I saw in 1948 were not fulfilled, I can still understand why, at the time, electroencephalograms seemed more relevant to psychiatry than did measures of hormones in urine.

Hoagland was a natural charmer. To me, he looked like a model of the aristocratic Old New England intellectual. He was tall, blade thin, had what are referred to as "finely chiseled features," and cut a very elegant figure when he drove from the Foundation to the state hospital in his convertible Aston-Martin with his Stetson hat. Later I learned that the family money came from his wife, who was the adopted daughter of old money. But Hoagland's charisma was all his own, and he charmed rich foundation donors and poor psychiatric residents indiscriminately.

Hoagland had been and always remained something of an intellectual dilettante, and that appealed to me too. For example, once his wife had a fever and sent Hoagland to the store for aspirin. When he returned, she scolded him for taking so long. Since she was a musician with an excellent sense of time, he wondered if her fever had distorted her internal clock. So he took her temperature, had her estimate a minute, and then gave her the aspirin. As her temperature fell, he had her make other estimates of a minute. When her temperature was normal he plotted the logarithm of her time estimations against the logarithm of her temperature. He found it was almost linear, and a good fit to the Arrhenius equation. That is the formula for the relationship between temperature and the rate of a chemical reaction. Pursuing that observation, he carried out a series of more controlled studies on the biology of time sense. For example, he took the diathermy machines, once used to produce fever for the treatment of central nervous system syphilis, and with them artificially raised and lowered the temperatures of normal subjects while he had them make time estimations. Again, he found that the hotter one is, the faster one's internal clock, and the slower real time seems to pass.

He correctly reasoned that enzyme systems were involved in time sense, but never guessed the true complexity. There is today a well-established branch of science known as chronobiology, which is concerned with the relations of biological systems and time. Now we know there are a number of *zeitgibers* or timekeepers in mammals. One of the most important of them involves the feedback loops between proteins and gene expression, which of course we knew nothing about in 1948.

I also remember Hoagland describing a study he once did with ants. He had kept a colony in one of those glass-walled ant cities where he could observe their behavior. He watched while the workers left the colony to forage for food and noted how they returned to feed the rest of the colony. While workers were foraging, a drop of peppermint oil near the food would send them scurrying back to the colony. He also observed the workers cleaning each other after such an episode, presumably to remove traces of the oil.

Then he blocked the entrance while a few peppermint-exposed ants were still outside. The locked-out ants seemed to become disorganized and milled about aimlessly. Then when the entrance was unblocked and the distressed workers regained the colony, instead of being cleaned by their fellow workers, they were quickly killed. He felt his animal study suggested that there were ancient roots for society's traditional hostility to schizophrenics, which manifested itself in the centuries of abuse endured by such individuals. In any case it made a neat metaphor for the prejudices against the mentally ill that we constantly encountered and struggled against.

It was Hoagland's charm, plus an episode that I will describe, that made me forgive him for his one glaring fault. He had a block on remembering names. I ran his EEG laboratory for him for almost two years, yet when a visiting dignitary would come around and he would start to introduce me, he would end up saying, "And this is, er, Noch, good old Noch." Rumor even had it that when the Worcester newspaper called to get details of his daughter's wedding, he could not remember the last name of his son-in-law to be.

But the event that reassured me the most that there was nothing personal about his inability to recall my last name came when the great neuropsychologist, Herbert Jasper, visited Worcester. Jasper and the neurosurgeon, Wilder Penfield, had done pioneering studies in Montreal on the localization of functions in the brain. So, Jasper was invited to give a talk at one of our hospital/foundation evening seminars. Hoagland had graciously included me in a pre-lecture dinner at the exclusive Worcester Club, and I do not know what I was enjoying the most, eating the Club's rare roast beef or listening to Jasper talk about his experiments on brain localization. Then I noticed Hoagland jotting something down in a notebook. Jasper was an old friend of Hoagland's and knew of his foible. Noticing what Hoagland was doing, he leaned over and in a stage whisper spelled out, "H-E-R-B-E-R-T J-A-S-P-E-R."

6

Are You There?

Early in my first year, I could not wait to learn more about these mysterious EEGs. Bill Houseman, a fellow resident, joined me in volunteering to work for Hoagland in the hospital EEG lab, and we worked together until Bill was called up for the Army Medical Corps reserves. The EEG machine was one of the first units Grass had manufactured. The pre-amps were battery powered, while the power amps could deliver 500 volts to the four big coils that drove the ink pens. Carelessness around the pen driver coils could have shocking consequences. So, we learned to replace the batteries, test vacuum tubes, troubleshoot the amplifiers, and build associated electronic gadgets.

We made our own electrodes by dropping a blob of hot solder on a plate of glass and then soldering the electrode wire to the dome of metal above the flattened base. We made our own electrode paste with bentonite, calcium chloride, and sodium chloride, and used that to stick the electrodes to the patient's scalp. To make a recording, the subject was placed on a bed in a chicken-coop-like frame cage made of unpainted 2x2 inch pine that had been covered with a screen of copper wire. The screen was carefully soldered at all the edges and connected to a cold water pipe ground so as to provide what is known as a Faraday shield. The purpose of such a shield is to absorb electrostatic fields. The 60 cycle fields generated by the 110-volt house electrical wiring was particularly pesky about causing interfering potentials in the subject and the electrodes, particularly if electrodes came loose.

We did routine EEGs for the hospital. The work was rewarding because we had plenty of patients with epilepsy, brain tumors, and head injuries. EEGs can be usefully diagnostic in such patients. We, of course, had regular, carefully considered, ongoing research projects. But Hoagland was always coming up with spur-of-the-moment experiments.

One of the first EEG phenomena described by Hans Berger, the discoverer of the EEG, was alpha blocking. Alpha is a rather regular 10-per-second electrical oscillation that can be recorded best from the occiput, or back, of the head. Alpha activity is strongest when the subject is alert but resting with eyes closed. It blocks, or disappears, to be replaced by lower voltage, higher frequency activity when the eyes are opened and visual processing is active.

Other electroencephalographers had published papers on alpha blocking during episodes of visual hallucination, so Hoagland had decided to see if auditory hallucinations were associated with brain wave changes. Speech frequencies lie between about 40 and 10,000 hertz (cycles per second). Since our pens could not record much above 20 hertz, loudspeakers were added to the ink pens so he could listen for activity in the 40-10,000 hertz range.

Hoagland found a cooperative patient who complained of frequent auditory hallucinations, so he hooked up the patient, put him in the shielded cage and asked him to lie quietly but to lift his right index finger when he began to hear the voices. Just as the patient's finger lifted, a voice came over the loudspeaker saying, "Hello, hello, are you there?" Hoagland told us that for a moment he wondered if he was actually hearing the patient's auditory hallucinations. But the voice continued, "Testing, testing, one two three, this is W1BA."

Apparently the ham radio station was so close that its magnetic fields were inducing currents in the patient and his electrodes. Faraday shields are not much protection from magnetic fields and the whole arrangement of patient and electrodes amounted to a huge crystal radio receiver.

One day, Hoagland asked us to help him out with another odd experiment. He apologized for the strange request, but said a chiropractor, who had made significant contributions to the foundation, wanted to see if brain waves changed when he manipulated the skull in ways intended to change the flow of cerebrospinal fluid. So Bill had his head massaged while I recorded his EEG. Nothing seemed to change, either subjectively or in the EEG, but the chiropractor was delighted with the respectful reception we gave to his ideas, and I hope he continued to contribute to the foundation. And I cannot imagine that Bill and myself would have turned down a request from Hoagland, no matter how outlandish it sounded.

7

Insulin Coma (aka Insulin Shock) Therapy

One consequence of my fascination with electroencephalograms was my introduction to insulin coma treatment. About halfway through my first year, Bill Hauseman was called up by the Army, and I became the default head electroencephalographer for the hospital. Of course Hoagland remained the official chief, but, ever the dilettante (and fund raiser), he was usually busy elsewhere. Over the preceding four months I had read almost everything worth reading about EEGs, although I must hasten to add that such a feat spoke more to the paucity of literature than to my rate of reading.

Since neurology and psychiatry were more closely allied in those days, we admitted epileptics and patients with brain tumors, so I had also done a fair amount of on-the-job learning in clinical electroencephalography. I had even come to consider myself quite the expert. Meanwhile, I spent any other free time reading psychoanalytic literature, as did most of my fellow residents.

Dr. David Rothschild, however, was less impressed with EEG's than I was, and one day he asked if, since I had the leisure to run the EEG lab, I might consider taking on the female insulin shock unit. So, ever eager for advancement, I gave myself a crash course on insulin shock therapy over the weekend, and on Monday at dawn began my tour of duty. Happily, I discovered my role was that of token physician and pupil, since the nurses on the unit were experienced and expert.

Insulin shock therapy was started in the 1930s when a German psychiatrist named Manfred Sakel observed that some diabetic schizophrenics who had suffered hypoglycemic comas from accidental insulin overdoses subsequently recovered from their schizophrenia. He elaborated that observation into a treatment, and his procedure was introduced into the United States when an authorized translation by Joe Wortis was published in 1938. Until the 1950s it was unquestionably the most effective treatment available for schizophrenia.

Controlled studies of insulin shock treatment had been done at Worcester just before my time, and they showed the treatment was effective, although much less so than its original practitioners had thought. In the 1950s, chlorpromazine, the first of the true antipsychotic drugs, was introduced. It was simpler to use, appeared less dangerous, and had a much clearer effect in modifying schizophrenia. So insulin shock slowly disappeared from the psychotherapeutic armamentarium, and vanished finally in the 1970s.

Insulin shock therapy began each day at around 6:00 A.M. when the patients were brought to the treatment area. The treatment was done six days a week, and each day the insulin dose for the new patient was slowly increased. Then, on subsequent days, using the dose of insulin needed by that particular patient, coma was induced and allowed to persist for up to an hour and a half. The comas were continued for a week or so, and then doses of insulin were reduced quickly over several days to terminate the treatment. Every patient was different, but usually each treatment was finished by noon, and within a week, a particular dose of insulin was found that would produce a full coma in any given new patient. This heroic procedure theoretically entailed considerable risk to the patient, but was amazingly safe in skilled hands. During my two years of association with insulin shock treatment, we never had a serious untoward reaction.

At 6:00 A.M., when the patients were brought to the unit, they were given a little tea and their injection of insulin. The unit was a large, bright room with six beds. Usually about four patients were treated at a time. After the injection of their coma-producing dose of insulin, the patient would get into bed and prepare for the descent into coma.

The first or induction phase started a few minutes after the injection of insulin, and was characterized by a feeling of hunger, some dizziness, and general relaxation. During this induction phase there could be a remarkable, if transient, clearing of the psychosis.

In the next phase after the injection, early coma developed, and there would be profuse sweating and sometimes mild agitation. It was said that, in this stage, some patients might have seizures and others might develop a sort of muscular rigidity. This latter condition was referred to as decerebrate rigidity because it resembled the rigidity seen when the connections between the brain and the lower brain stem structures are cut. Seizures and decerebrate rigidity were considered reasons to terminate the coma immediately. Incidentally, I never witnessed an insulin shock patient have a seizure or exhibit decerebrate rigidity.

The last stage was reached when, with a full dose of insulin, a deep coma developed. In that stage, consciousness was completely lost and muscles became flaccid. After 90 minutes of coma, the treatment was terminated by administering sugar. We always tried first to pass a nasogastric tube. We made a careful check to be sure we were in the stomach by withdrawing some fluid content and testing it with litmus paper. If the paper indicated a strong acid, we could be pretty sure the tube was in the right place. Then we would introduce a heavily sugared solution directly into the stomach.

With luck, the patient would wake up enough to drink sugared orange juice, then eat a meal and return to the ward. Sometimes, however, when tube feeding did not arouse the patient, an intravenous injection was required. Getting 50 c.c. of heavy syrup injected into veins, which were often collapsed, was no mean feat, but fortunately the nurses were experts, and I learned.

After the coma was terminated, the patient was returned to the ward, where he or she was given frequent feedings while the attendants watched like a hawk for the sweating and confusion that signaled a late recurrence of hypoglycemia (low blood sugar).

Insulin shock therapy never even remotely resembled the horrendous procedure depicted in the otherwise wonderful movie, *A Beautiful Mind*, which was based on a biography of Nobel Prize Laureate John Nash. In one scene, the actor portraying Nash was forcibly restrained, and screamed in terror before convulsing. Now, in her book *A Beautiful Mind*[1] on which that movie was based, Silvia Nasar wrote that John Nash was given insulin shock therapy. In a talk she later gave at Stanford University, she reported that Nash, on seeing the movie, remarked that he could not remember ever having had any therapy like that. Of course he could not remember such a treatment since he never had it.

For a time there was indeed a convulsive treatment that used the seizure-producing drug, pentamethylenetetrazol, also called Metrazol, and that did produce reactions like those shown in the movie. But authentic insulin shock therapy was apparently too un-dramatic for Hollywood. Today, lies that the film industry tells about insulin shock therapy are irrelevant, because, happily, we do not need to use that treatment any more. Unfortunately, in the case of electroconvulsive therapy, the way Hollywood has demonized and dramatized it still makes things tough when a patient really needs that particular treatment. I will return to the subject of electroconvulsive therapy later, in Chapter 9.

But back to my personal memories. On rare occasions a patient would, despite every precaution, lapse into coma in the middle of the night. The night staff was not so expert and on such occasions the "duty" resident had to manage things. While calls for treating midnight hypoglycemic attacks were not frequent, they were common enough to have left a lasting impression on me. Before we moved into the hospital, I stayed in the residents' bedroom when I had the duty, and getting me up for a medical emergency was no problem. After we moved to a room in the hospital, they simply came in our bedroom to get me. While it seemed that everything else in the hospital had a lock and key, our bedrooms did not.

The night attendant, not bothering to knock, would simply open the door, shine a flashlight on us and say, "Need you quick, Doc!" Thus I, and my fellow residents who lived in the hospital, were almost as open to unannounced observation as were our patients.

My wife, Dorothy, never quite got used to the lack of privacy, but it could have been worse. Bob Simmonson, a fellow resident, got married during his second year and was awarded a fine bedroom in the hospital. One of the housekeepers was a semi-patient who was allowed to keep working although deaf, almost blind, and mildly demented. One morning when the newlyweds were having intercourse, that poor housekeeper came in and began making the bed, oblivious of the fact that she was causing *coitus interruptus*.

8

By These Signs Shall Ye Know Them

Other than doors to staff bedrooms, all doors at Worcester were usually locked and could only be opened with a huge key. As a consequence, all members of the staff had a ring full of these keys, which they attached to their belts by strong leashes, so the keys could not be snatched away by patients. The keys and their corresponding keyholes were so big that there was no need to fiddle around finding a keyhole in the dark, or in an emergency.

These keys were a part of all our lives. We joked that the keys had to be so large because they served as a kind of uniform and were the only sure way one could tell patients apart from staff. In those days, attending physicians wore long white coats and house staff wore short white coats. Nurses, occupational therapists, and attendants had an elaborate cap symbolism with shape indicating status and whether one was registered. In the case of graduate (registered) nurses, there were also pins and colored decorations which showed where they had been trained. But visiting staff and consultants wore street suits, so the keys were the only true guarantee of non-patient status.

To the outsider, the huge key rings gave the place a formidable look, and invited comparison of the staff to jailers in a prison. In point of fact, the staff did not feel that they were jailers. The great iron gates in the surrounding stone wall were never closed, and the idea that a staff of a few hundred could keep over 3,000 inmates imprisoned was absurd. Many of the wards were open in the daytime, so that patients could come and go with varying amounts of supervision. Most of the patients on the locked wards were so disturbed that they could not take care of themselves on the outside. Never more than a handful of patients posed active suicide risks or physical threats to society.

On the other hand, the keys were in fact status symbols. I remember once particular instance when the symbolism of the keys received a dramatic affirmation. There was a neurology resident doing his psychiatric rotation at Worcester who was, even by our relaxed standards, a very odd fellow. He was one of those blondes that seem almost transparent. He parted his hair around the back of his head, about where the pathologist cuts the scalp for opening the skull at postmortem, and then combed it all forward. He said he hated to feel wet, so when he showered he did it quickly, and then dumped talcum powder over himself. The curious back-parted and powdered hairdo definitely set him apart from the crowd.

My friend and fellow resident, Bill Hauseman, tended to be a bit more conservative than I was and quickly categorized him as, "Weird, even for a neurologist." However, other than his odd appearance, I found the neurology resident to be a bright fellow with an amiable disposition. There was only one other thing about him that I remember as being a bit unusual. He collected gold coins and once showed me his framed displays. The coins that he showed me had to be worth a small fortune, or so it seemed to me in those days, and I thought it odd that he would bring them with him for a month's rotation at a state hospital. Of course I knew that Freud had attributed both collecting things and odd bath habits to fixation at the anal stage of development, but then the Freudians found psychopathology in everyone.

There was a joke, current in those days, about a patient on his way to his analyst. He ran into a friend who asked, "Why so sad looking?"

The patient replied, "It's my analyst. He always makes me feel bad. If I'm late I'm hostile, if I'm on time I'm obsessive, and if I'm early I'm anxious."

But back to the odd-looking neurologist. One evening, he went down to a ward to make a quick note in a chart, and absentmindedly left his keys in his room. A nurse who knew him was leaving just as he entered the locked unit, so she held the door open for him. Thus he did not notice that he had no keys when he came on the ward. But, by the time he had finished making his notes, the night shift had arrived and there was no longer any staff member around who knew him.

He approached the night head nurse and explained his keyless-ness, but she was unimpressed. After finally finding a patient who would vouch for him, he got the nurse to reluctantly allow him one phone call. Fortunately, he was able to get a fellow resident on the phone, but the nurse insisted the psychiatric resident personally come and take charge of the unfortunate neurologist.

This episode struck me as particularly amusing, but of course this was not the only time a staff member was misidentified as a patient. I suppose the moral could be, "While people should not judge books by their covers, they do, so it is wise to watch your cover."

9

Electroconvulsive Therapy (ECT)

Most of us residents shared an abiding faith that releasing repressed hostility through skillful psychotherapy would cure any depression. Hence, sending a patient for electroconvulsive therapy, known variously as ECT and electric shock therapy, was tantamount to a confession of therapeutic incompetence. Of course, ECT has always had bad press. The very name sounds brutal, and misleading. Fiction sensationalizing mental institutions, like *One Flew over the Cuckoo's Nest* by Ken Kesey,[2] have not helped.

The fact is that ECT is still probably the fastest and surest way to treat depression. After treatment, some patients do complain of lost memories, but this is not always the case. Besides, chronic depression impairs memory, and has been found to reduce the number of neurons in the hippocampus, which is a part of the brain that plays a crucial role in memory. Otherwise, the so-called "associated adverse events" are less than with any other antidepressant therapy available even today. Also, in the days before antipsychotic drugs and potent muscle relaxing agents like dantrolene, ECT was lifesaving in cases of malignant catatonia, where the extreme muscle spasms may produce an overheating (i.e., hyperthermia) that can be fatal.

These days, ECT is a very civilized procedure. The patient is given an anesthetic and an airway is established so that oxygen can be given. The EEG is recorded so the operator can tell when a seizure has been induced. With the patient asleep, his muscles are paralyzed with a curare-like drug, so there is no physical convulsion. The patient is ventilated with oxygen because so long as the muscles are paralyzed, there is no spontaneous breathing. Then an electrical current with electronically controlled waveform and duration is passed through the head to produce an electrical seizure in the brain, which is verified by the EEG. After the seizure ends, artificial ventilation is maintained until spontaneous breathing returns. Then the patient is put into a recovery room until fully conscious. The whole procedure is no worse than going under a general anesthetic, as for example in a colonoscopy.

In my days as a resident, I will admit that the procedure was more formidable than its modern version. The patient lay on a table with pillows placed to minimize the risk of a compression fracture of the spine. A tongue blade wrapped with gauze was placed between his teeth to reduce the risk of breaking a tooth during the convulsion. The temples were wiped with a salt paste and the electrodes were held on the head with wooden calipers. The shock-box consisted of a variable transformer so the voltage could be controlled, and a spring-operated timer switch to control the duration. One set the time and voltage for that particular patient and pushed the button. The patient gave a kind of groan, and then went into a tonic spasm with back arched and the torso lifted off the table. That was followed by the rhythmically jerking clonic spasm. The attendants held on to the arms and legs gingerly, because a limb could be broken if too much force was exerted against the convulsive movements. The patient did not breathe during the seizure, but the anoxia was not clinically significant, because breathing started again promptly after the seizure, and well before consciousness returned.

There was a room set aside with mattresses covering its floor. Once the seizure was over, the unconscious patient was carried to that room and put on the mattresses until consciousness returned. Following the period of unconsciousness, there would be a period referred to as post-ictal (*ictus* = seizure) confusion when the patient would toss and turn. The mattresses on the floor were used because we did not have enough hospital beds with side rails, or enough attendants to keep patients from falling out of ordinary beds. Then, when the patient was steady enough to stand and walk, he would be led back to his own bed to complete his recovery.

The effectiveness of shock treatment was undeniable. Yet, facts and our personal observations to the contrary, we residents had more faith in our psychotherapy than we did in ECT. Of course, some depressions respond to psychotherapy, and many depressions, even some psychotic ones, remit spontaneously. So we all had our cures to brag about. Most of all, we were convinced that, since hidden unexpressed hostility lay at the root of every depression, it only needed the therapist's skill to drain the festering rage. Then we would see health restored by our deep compassion and penetrating insights.

As for the effectiveness of ECT, there is one patient I particularly remember. I will refer to him with the fictitious name Donald Dunner. He was the business administrator for a religious organization. He and his wife were childless, but they lived a happy life united in their faith and in their good works. When Donald was about 45, he began to worry that he was making mistakes in his bookkeeping. Several audits showed him to be almost unbelievably meticulous, but he could not be reassured. He became sleepless and cried often. He repeatedly told his wife and his pastor that he was a bad person. He knew he had done something evil, only he did not know what it was. Then, one night he tried to hang himself. His suicide attempt was a workman-like job, and only some unsuspected dry rot in a basement beam saved his life.

When he was admitted as my patient, I knew I could help him. He had sandy hair, a stocky build, and was in great physical shape, but was tearful and obviously miserable. While he could recall nothing but a life devoted to his church and its charities, he was sure there was some hidden sin. I concurred, for such unremitting virtue could only be explained by deeply repressed hostility. I saw him five days a week for an hour at a time while he lost weight, sobbed, and thanked me for my efforts. At the end of a month when he came up for staff review, Dr. Rothschild asked me if I thought I was making progress. When I confessed that I did not think so, he said, "Well, Dr. Callaway, would you consider ECT?"

I told the chief that I was meeting with Donald and his wife the next day and would discuss it with them. At the meeting, they reassured me that I was the most wonderful physician on earth and that they would consent to whatever I suggested. And so I gave Donald ECT, feeling every bit a total failure.

After the second treatment, Donald was clearly better. On the weekend following his third treatment, he went for a ride with his wife, and, after three weeks, he went home on a trial visit that ended in his discharge. Donald was well but I felt I had failed.

For years I continued to get cards and small gifts of thanks from Donald. Then one day I got a long letter from his wife. Donald had died of a sudden heart attack, but she thanked me for the wonderful years they had enjoyed together, as the result of the remarkable care I had provided during his nervous breakdown.

10

The Last Resort

Lobotomies were done at the hospital by Dr. Carmody, a neurosurgeon, who would come down from Boston for the occasion. First year residents were assigned in rotation to serve as his assistant surgeon, but other than the physical discomfort of assisting at an interminable neurosurgical procedure with a meticulous operator, it was not so bad. He was a gentleman and perhaps unique among neurosurgeons of that era because he never raised his voice or insulted others in the operating room. He had trained under one of the early gods of neurosurgery whose abuses of staff, both physical and verbal, were legendary. As a resident, he had sworn that when he finished his training, no one in his operating room would ever be hurt or humiliated. I was hardly the most dexterous of surgeons, but he always made me feel good about my efforts.

There was always a lot of soul searching before the staff recommended a lobotomy, and then there were further reviews at the state level because of the cost. Of course, psychosurgery went totally against the grain of the psychoanalytic zeitgeist that all the residents embraced. We had ample evidence of the effectiveness of lobotomy all around us, but we also could observe the undesirable side effects, or "associated adverse events," as they say in current psychopharmacological techno-speak.

For example, the frontal lobes were supposed to be involved with morals and conscience, and those virtues were thought to be damaged by lobotomy. One of our brilliant successes had been a very disturbed schizophrenic. After his lobotomy, he was discharged and became a prominent Boston politician. We speculated that perhaps here was a situation where an associated adverse event, in this case an attenuation of moral concerns, was not adverse so far as success in the outside world was the criterion. Even today, morals and conscience do not seem essential to a career in politics.

Mary Burns was another case in point. Before her operation, her hands were raw and bleeding from her compulsive hand washing. Even when restrained from washing, her constant whining made her a real nuisance.

During a year of futile psychotherapy, her people outside the hospital closed ranks and she became a woman with no family or home. Finally, and perhaps too late, a lobotomy was authorized. The results were miraculous, and she could have been discharged if she could have had minimal supervision outside the hospital. The adverse effect of this generally positive lobotomy was a difficulty stopping something once she had started. Although clearly much improved, she could not leave the hospital without someone to set limits. So she stayed on at the hospital, did housework at the homes of the senior staff, and received a small salary.

Unfortunately, the adverse event associated with her lobotomy had consequences that, on one occasion, were particularly distressing to the house staff. The wife of the senior staff physician on the female side had planned to have a lasagna feed for the perpetually malnourished house staff. It was to be on a Sunday evening when the staff dining room was closed and the junior staff ate in the patient's cafeteria. Late in the afternoon before the lasagna party, and after taking four beautiful pans of lasagna out of the oven, the wife of the senior staff physician left to make a quick trip to the grocery for some forgotten items.

In the meantime, Mary Burns dropped in to help serve the party. When the doctor's wife returned, she found Mary in tears and the four lasagna pans sitting empty on the kitchen table. "I'm so sorry." Mary sobbed. "I was just going to taste one and once I started I could not stop!"

The doctor's wife had Gurrey, the switchboard operator, spread news of the disaster among the residents and their wives. That night we all went down to the patients' cafeteria with heavy hearts. I wonder where the hospital got the cold cuts they served on Sunday evenings. They had an ineffable "not-quite-right" taste, and to this day I retain an aversion to cold cuts.

11

Beauty Is As Beauty Does

Prejudice is a dirty word in California in the third millennium. It is like halitosis. People find it offensive. They will not tell you what is wrong to your face but will talk about you behind your back. On the other hand, as a student of human brain-mind issues, I must say that our brains seemed designed to function on prejudices, and it is just those prejudices that allow our brains to make statistically useful conclusions on the basis of inadequate data. One of my mentors observed that if someone claimed to be unprejudiced, that person was either naïve (without experience), or a liar, or more often both. The trick is to recognize our prejudices, modify them by experience, and exercise them with compassion.

I knew a psychologist who worked in the department of mental retardation. She spent most of her time doing intelligence tests of what were known as FLKs (funny looking kids). It was not unusual for her to find normal and even superior intelligence in kids that were institutionalized because they were so ugly and dumb looking. Just as we expect dumb and ugly to go together, we expect the beautiful to be bright.

A 1962 movie called *The Light in the Piazza* became a Broadway play. The story concerns an upper class mother devoting her life to caring for a gorgeous daughter who had suffered some brain damage as the result of a horseback riding accident. Daughter and mother end up in Italy, where the gentle but none too bright son of a well-to-do family falls in love with the daughter. The young man proposes, and the mother reluctantly gives the marriage her blessing in the face of strong opposition from her husband. The boy and girl are wed, the big, extended Italian family accepts her warmly, and her brain damage doesn't stop her from fitting right in with the other women who do little more than look at fashion magazines, discuss makeup, and have babies.

When I saw the movie, I was put in mind of Helen, the sister of a girl named Mary Lou, whom I dated prior to my engagement and marriage to Dorothy. Mary Lou was cute, bright (she later published a novel), and might have passed as beautiful but for Helen, who looked like a friendly

Hedy Lamar. Helen could say the rote things a well-bred Southern lady was expected to say, but other than that she simply smiled, groomed herself, and looked smashing.

When I had been dating Mary Lou for a while, and we were sharing more intimate things, she confided in me that her parents were worried sick about Helen, her retarded sister. It had never occurred to me that Helen was retarded until Mary Lou mentioned it. However, I cannot imagine that some hunting and golfing Southern gentleman with servants and money would not marry her. Her beauty, good manners, good blood lines, and mental retardation would have made her an ideal mate for his sort.

This brings me to the strange story of Jan, who was not so lucky. Her husband died and, while she had a sister and a daughter who were concerned about her, no one thought to help with her finances, so soon they were nonexistent. She apparently made periodic appearances at various New England hospital emergency rooms but reconstituted quickly so no one ever gave her a second thought. For reasons that were never clear to me, she made two visits in a row to the emergency room at the general hospital in Worcester. On her second visit, her strange clinical picture generated enough interest to get her transferred to us.

I met her when she arrived at Worcester State Hospital, and she indeed presented us with a puzzling picture. She was well-groomed and well-spoken. At 40, she was still a very beautiful woman. On admission she was obviously very frightened, but could not give a good explanation as to why that was so. She had some vague paranoid ideas about people who wanted to hurt her. She was so panicked and agitated that I put her in a quiet or seclusion room. After an hour she calmed down and thanked me for the protection she sensed. Then we had a conversation that had not the slightest hint of schizophrenia in it. At times she appeared drowsy, lost the thread of our discussion, and smiled in a sweetly apologetic way. I attributed that to Jan's prior sleep loss.

Jan's supportive family was there the next morning. Her daughter said Jan had always been odd. Most of the time while the daughter was growing, Jan simply lay in bed looking gorgeous. By the next day, Jan looked fine and I could have discharged her. But we were not under modern constraints on length of hospital stay, and everyone thought a few more days of study could not hurt, as it had become clear that this was not the first of the odd panic attacks.

I began working her up diligently and coming up empty handed. Her EEG (including recordings with the new nasopharangeal lead that I had gotten from Harvard) was unremarkable. I dug deep and considered the adrenal tumor called pheochromacytoma. This is a rare condition where a tumor composed of adrenal cells can put out bursts of adrenaline, with resulting panic attacks. However I knew I was clutching at straws since her lifelong history of odd behavior pretty well ruled that out. I studied her urine for porphyrins, a sort of chemical that results from a rare metabolic disorder and that can be associated with transient psychoses. After finding no porphyrins in Jan's urine, Dr. Rothschild, the Clinical Director, suggested a full battery of psychological tests. Outside, that would have cost thousands of dollars, since a full battery of psychological tests involved over 10 hours of testing and about the same amount of time for analysis. However, with all the clinical psychology students at Worcester State Hospital, the only question was who would get to do the testing.

I was wondering about temporal epilepsy in spite of the normal EEG, and so I particularly requested a Luria battery, which was supposed to pick up signs of temporal epilepsy.

Jan, meanwhile, happily worked away in our beautifully equipped occupational therapy suite. The occupational therapists often competed with the psychologists in making diagnostic inferences, and so just before I got the psychological report, one of the occupational therapists came to me and said, "Jan is doing good work in all areas, but at the level of a six-year-old." That didn't really sink in, because right after the occupational therapist left, the psychologist walked into my office.

"Guess what we found?" she said, looking very pleased with herself.

"The Luria shows temporal epilepsy?" I speculated hopefully.

"No," the psychologist continued, "but guess what her IQ is?"

"90," I hazarded. While I had never guessed Jan was clinically retarded, I knew she was no rocket scientist

"70," the psychologist said proudly. "And not much spread between performance and verbal."

That absence of spread suggested that Jan had always been just the way she was now. People develop their vocabularies early in life, and they remain very resistant to brain disease. If you are retarded during your vocabulary-learning years, you will always have a retarded vocabulary. Problems, both physical and psychological, that come up later in life, depress performance scores more than verbal scores. Patients even retain their old vocabularies when they cannot learn new words, cannot copy simple figures, etc. So it looked like Jan was just on the very low end of the distribution curve. Her bizarre panic attacks apparently happened when the routine of ordinary life overwhelmed this unfortunate lady.

After some discussion between family and staff, we all decided on a paid companion. At the time it seemed the best of possible solutions. How that worked out in the end I am afraid I do not know. But once again my preconceptions (that sounds better than to say my prejudices) had kept me from seeing a simple truth that was right in front of me. I wish I could say that was the last time. But I do not think I was ever so misled by a pretty face again.

12

Some Comments on the Subject of Schizophrenia

The word schizophrenia literally means split (*schizo*) and brain (*phrenos*). Like much else associated with this dreadful condition, that name just confuses and does not make the slightest contribution to either our understanding or our therapeutic efforts. Since schizophrenia will feature in so many of these reminiscences, you may reasonably ask, "What is schizophrenia?" The short answer is, "I don't know."

When I was at Worcester State Hospital, the *Worcester Times* ran an article on the hospital with lots of pictures. The title was "People Just Like Us." However well meaning the reporter was, he lied. Those who need asylum do so precisely because they are not like us, and among those who need asylum, the schizophrenics are the most UN-like us.

Earlier, I referred to the movie *A Beautiful Mind*. The film may have erred in its portrayal of insulin shock treatment, but the director-poet captures things that I can only marvel at and in most cases affirm. Take the horror of the episode when Nash's devoted wife gets mixed into his delusional system and he tries to kill her.

Too often, those of us in this field have watched helplessly while parents, distraught and baffled by the sinister transformations in their most promising child, spend fruitless hours trying to reason the child out of his or her delusions.

In my days as a resident, besides having the intellectual advantage of observing the natural course of untreated diseases, we were not under any insurance-driven compulsion to name everything, as though we knew what we were talking about. Among our schizophrenic patients, there were some who sank slowly and irretrievably into dementia praecox (i.e. premature dementia), and there were some who recovered completely with no more episodes.

Les Philips, the chief psychologist at Worcester, discovered one of the few prognostic signs for schizophrenia, but it held only for males.

The better the pre-psychotic psycho-sexual relationships of the patient, the better the prognosis. None of the clinical symptoms such as catatonia, paranoia, etc. that one saw during an acute episode turned out to have any useful predictive value. Of course, the longer the patient was sick, the smaller the probability of recovery was, but that recovery probability seemed never to go to zero. Some of our best descriptions of this illness come from autobiographies and biographies but they, almost by definition, have to do with the remitting form of the disease.

While I may not know what schizophrenia is, I have a pretty good idea of what schizophrenia is not. For example, it is not like most psychoses caused by the drugs we once called psychotomimetic (psychosis mimicking), such as lysergic acid di-ethyl amide and peyote. In fact, those drugs are now called psychodelic (the current *in*-word, from the Greek roots *psyche* = mind and *delos* = manifesting). Some people, experimenting with mind-altering drugs, experience a terror when perceptions they had taken for granted become bizarre and unreliable. While this mental malaise and confusion is suggestive of some schizophrenias, clinicians are rarely fooled by reactions to psychedelic drugs. In addition, schizophrenics who have taken psychedelics during remissions from real schizophrenia have told me that the drug-induced experience and the illness are very different. In a way, this is unfortunate; many of us wasted a good deal of time studying psychedelics with the idea they would shed some light on schizophrenia.

Some schizophrenics do go through episodes of delirium, and for a time that may look like any other delirium. I was once fooled by a patient who turned out to have acute encephalitis. If one waits, the situation will usually become clearer, but failure to diagnosis some of the rare, potentially confusing, and also potentially treatable deliria can leave the patient to experience unnecessary suffering.

However, most toxic deliria are not confusing. Consider the trembling delirium (*delirium tremens* or DTs) that happens when a heavy drinker abruptly stops drinking. There is a story (probably untrue, but illustrative none the less) of playful German psychiatric residents who slipped a white laboratory rabbit into the room of a patient with DTs who was sitting on the floor counting hallucinated black rabbits. The patient continued his counting, "41, 42, 43, that SOB is white, 45, 46. . ."

For the counter story, a paranoid schizophrenic said a cowled monk passed her window every night at the stroke of midnight. She drew pictures of the monk, his hood, and generally described him in detail. So one of the residents dressed up exactly according to her descriptions, and at the stroke of midnight, while the other residents waited with the patient, he walked past her window. The assembled residents exclaimed, "We see your monk!"

"That is not my monk," She said. Then, pointing just behind the departing impersonation of her hallucination, she exclaimed: "There is my monk!"

Doctors have always used words to obscure things. Eponyms (Dorothy Reed cells for Hodgkin's sarcoma) and words from dead languages (*icthiosis* for fish-scale-like skin) have traditionally helped physicians shroud their thinking in mystery, not only to enhance the apparent wisdom of doctors, but also to shield the patient when physicians speculate about potential bad news. In addition, such private language helps physicians avoid facing their own ignorance. Schizophrenia is a word that has served that last unfortunate function without having either of the first two questionable virtues.

Currently, clinical self-deception is further abetted by statistical pseudo-descriptions. A look at the current standard psychiatric *Diagnosis and Statistical Manual*[3] (DSM IV is on my desk at the moment) will show that its definitions of psychiatric diseases have become like the old Chinese restaurant menus. For a given price the menu might read as follows:

Select two from the following:

1. Fried Won Tons
2. Egg Rolls
3. Pot Stickers
4. Egg Drop Soup

For schizophrenia, DSM IV reads as follows:

A. Characteristic symptoms: Two (or more) from the following, each present for a significant portion of time during a 1-month period (or less if successfully treated):

1. Delusions;
2. Hallucinations;
3. Disorganized speech (e.g., frequent derailment or incoherence);
4. Grossly disorganized or catatonic behavior;
5. Negative symptoms. These include affective flattening, alogia (absence of logic) and avolition (reduced volition, or inability to initiate actions).

DSM IV continues with exclusionary criteria, which can be rephrased as: "If the disorder is brief or if you can make another diagnosis, then it is not schizophrenia." That sort of thing is quite useful for statistical purposes, and for inter-rater reliability in research projects. Such cut-and-dried definitions give the impression that one knows what one is talking about. They not only mask the mystery of the disease, but in addition, they foster the idea that we know what we are talking about, which could not be further from the truth.

Half a century ago, when we thought of schizophrenia, we looked for Manfred Bleuler's three A's: Autism, Ambivalence, and Affect (inappropriate). We tried to rule out syphilis, myxedema (thyroid deficiency), encephalitis (inflammation of the brain, usually due to a virus), pellagra (deficiency of B vitamins, especially thiamin), black widow spider bites, methamphetamine abuse, brain tumors, etc. We tried to separate out bipolar affective disorders (manic-depressives), but that was not, and still is not, always so obvious. Sometimes one has to watch the response to drugs to make a diagnosis, which is just backwards from the medical ideal where diagnosis determines treatment. After all this, what is left over is schizophrenia. Obviously such a residual category is likely to include a variety of disorders. In passing, it is interesting that "antipsychotics" are highly non-specific and find use in a variety of conditions that are not schizophrenia.

Often remissions in schizophrenia are as mysterious as the disease, and I will return to those puzzling phenomena later. Some seem related to physical stress. During my residency, and before drugs clouded the clinical pictures, emergency surgeries, such as appendectomies or hernia operations, were often associated with remission, as were attacks of asthma. We occasionally did Amytal interviews to get information from mute catatonics, and often the first injection of the barbiturate sedative occasioned a dramatic remission. Curiously, such Amytal remissions could never be induced a second time in schizophrenic patients. Equally unexplained are reports that repeated treatment with benzodiazepines, which today replace the barbiturates as sedatives, can sometimes produce a repeated remission from catatonia. So there you have some flavor of the mystery.

But I can close on a hopeful note. Modern genetic work suggests that there are several genotypes (genetic variations) associated with vulnerability to schizophrenia and that they interact in various ways with each other and with various environmental factors, for example low birth weight. In addition, subtle phenotypes (variations observable in individuals, such as abnormalities in startle reflexes and eye tracking) may be related to vulnerability and to a particular genotype. A search for abnormalities in the genome of an individual will soon be something the practicing clinician can have done, so the future looks bright. But imagine if you will a disease that is the result of interactions of at least four unrelated genetic factors and four unrelated environmental factors. If something like that is the case, then you can understand why I don't know what schizophrenia is.

13

We May Be Crazy But
We're Not Stupid

At Worcester, of all of the brilliant teachers I have been exposed to, my best instructors were my patients. Things I learned from my patients have endured over the years. This was augmented at Worcester because we lived almost side by side with the people we were trying to help, and knew them in ways that went beyond the less intimate, more professional doctor-patient relationships. And so this next story has to do with one of the first schizophrenics I came to know well.

Bill Smith was one of those tragic individuals who had been a real winner in high school. As a star athlete and student, he had gone to a prestigious college on a scholarship, and then developed schizophrenia in his freshman year. He was physically attractive, very bright, and wildly delusional. He had what we called a disorganized paranoid system. That is to say he thought some vaguely identified group was plotting against him and doing bizarre things to him. He also suffered from distressing auditory hallucinations from time to time. I tried to do psychotherapy with him.

I read everything I could get my hands on, and spent hours listening to him. He had failed to improve after a course of insulin shock treatments, and if my attempts to help him continued to be ineffectual, then he was doomed to the more custodial setting of a back ward. Over several months we developed a good personal relationship. He seemed to appreciate my efforts, and I learned a lot about him and his past, and also about his hallucinations and delusions.

According to what I had been led to believe from my readings, his onset of schizophrenia at age 21 simply did not make sense. He had been anything but the typical schizoid pre-schizophrenic. He had been popular and outgoing as a boy. While his family was not perfect, it seemed, if anything, less dysfunctional than my own. Bill and I worked hard, but his illness baffled both of us, and proved unresponsive to our best efforts.

Finally, Dr. Rothschild suggested I could put my energies to better use and Bill was moved to the second floor.

While the walls of the hospital were made of massive stone blocks, most of the floors were of linoleum-covered wood. Thus, fire was a real concern, and periodic fire drills were carried out. On the disturbed wards, patients were lined up at doors and then returned to their rooms, but the general confusion was not reassuring when one contemplated what might happen in an actual fire.

Then one day we had the real thing. On Bill's second floor, smoke began to seep out under the door of a linen room. Later, we learned that it was a rather minor fire, but when someone had opened the closet door to see what was going on, thick smoke had billowed out on to the ward. Fire alarms sounded and we had to cope with what seemed like a major fire.

In almost no time at all, rather frightened looking firemen were rushing on to the ward while the patients queued up and filed out into the courtyard. A few of the more intact patients acted crazy to spook the firemen, but most of them appeared quite sane. Patients who had been hallucinating, posturing, and in general behaving like lunatics are supposed to behave, suddenly acted entirely rationally. They quietly lined up, and marched out like well-drilled soldiers.

Once in the safety of the courtyard, and with word that the linen room fire had been extinguished, psychotic behavior began to be exhibited once again. I was helping out in the courtyard and found myself standing next to Bill.

"I'm impressed with the way you guys handled the fire," I said.

Bill smiled and replied, "We may be crazy, Doc, but we're not stupid!"

My exchange with Bill is not unique. Others have commented on how schizophrenics, who seem to be totally at the mercy of their psychoses, manage to master their madness when their survival is at stake. Some people writing about their own schizophrenic psychoses tell that, at times, the descent into psychosis has a voluntary aspect.

Consider a schizophrenic who is in remission on medication and who stops the medication deliberately, choosing instead the comforts of grandiose delusions. In such a case, is the patient at fault, and not simply the innocent victim of an illness? Such questions can lead to endless debates about determinism versus free will. Practically, such considerations complicate the theoretical and philosophical underpinnings of society's plans to treat schizophrenia, including the issue of involuntary medication.

As for Bill, I lost touch with him for about a year and a half. Then I ran into him by chance as I was passing through his ward. In that brief encounter Bill looked worse and did not acknowledge that he recognized me. I was told his parents still visited, clinging to the slim chance that Bill might make one of those unexplainable recoveries. One always hopes for the best, but the odds for Bill were getting pretty slim.

14

My Exhibitionism Gets a Lucky Break

Being a student was about the only role I knew from the time I was born until I graduated from medical school. After getting my Doctorate of Medicine, I naturally began looking forward to a parallel graduation from student to teacher. But the roots of deep longings usually have origins pre-dating conscious memories, and maybe even arise at the genomic level.

My father loved to teach, and had wanted to work in academic medicine. He made do by teaching as an ordained Episcopal lay reader and as an instructor at the local women's college. In my family, all teachers were held in great regard. So there you have one factor (definitely environmental and potentially genetic) in my desire to teach.

But equally important was the fact that, as an only child (for most of nine years), showing off (the result of my inherent narcissism) was so rewarded that a certain amount of exhibitionism was inevitable. And so, as is the case with many, if not most teachers, exhibitionism played a role in my teaching urge.

As an intern, we had medical students we could teach (on the rare occasions when we had moments to spare). But one of the things I loved about Worcester was being officially assigned to teach.

Sometimes it was a disaster. For example, I was sent to give a lecture on child rearing at the Worcester Women's Club. I had no experience with child rearing, but was undaunted because I was full of psychoanalytic theories on the subject. I was sure my great theoretical background would be valuable to those poor benighted mothers. Of course, they politely tore me limb from limb.

Sometimes I was apparently more successful. I taught the elements of EEGs to medical students, and later was elated when a famous neurologist told me that my teaching had been a major factor in her career choice. That particular neurologist is a very generous lady, but I prefer to take her compliment at face value.

Then there was the lucky incident that happened to me when I was giving the student nurses a course on psychoanalytic theory. By then

I knew enough to make sure my students knew less than I did, but I was taking them through the developmental stages and had entranced them with my discussion of oral conflicts. My next lecture had to do with anal development, and related obsessive compulsive symptoms. I described the anal triad of cleanliness, punctuality, and stinginess with examples. Then in closing, I added that when there were neurotic symptoms, their opposites had usually found hidden expression. For example, a compulsively clean person may keep a desk drawer full of dirty handkerchiefs.

My charming, energetic students used the night shift to explore the desk of a frighteningly clean head nurse, and low and behold, they found the handkerchiefs as advertised. Most of the students hailed me as a genius, but some whispered that I had planted the drawer (which of course I hadn't).

Thus, in treatment as in teaching, a little luck helps. I remember advice from one of my teachers. He said, "You'll be blamed for the failures due to chance, so enjoy the praise that you get by chance."

15

Truth Serum

During World War II, great claims were made for narcosynthesis. Soldiers suffering from combat fatigue were given intravenous injections of short acting barbiturate sedatives such as Amytal (sodium amobarbital) and interviewed while intoxicated. They would be encouraged to relive the traumatic experiences while sedated by the short-acting barbiturate. This process of reliving the past was referred to as abreaction. Then, with the help of a therapist, they would theoretically master and integrate the traumatic experience into the healthy part of their personalities. I was under the impression that the procedure fell out of favor in subsequent United States military engagements and was replaced by a gentler working through of traumatic experiences. Rather than using a drug to blast open the memories, the patient was encouraged to recount his traumatic experience, but was allowed to proceed at his own pace.

Recent studies have found that debriefing (talking to a counselor about a traumatic experience right after the event) does not help and may predispose people to later post traumatic stress disorders (PTSD). The unmodified re-experiencing of anxiety in debriefing may however be quite different from the Amytal interview, and some studies suggest that the immediate use of beta-adrenergic antagonists (e.g. propranalol), which dampen the autonomic effects of the trauma, can prevent some PTSDs. On the other hand, there seems to have been no deliberate comparison of Amytal interviews with more conventional psychotherapy, and no long term follow up of soldiers treated either way. To add a final note of confusion, a correspondent of mine who was a medical officer in Vietnam recalls the regular and acutely effective use of Amytal interviews in combat zones.

Amytal was also hailed as "truth serum." It was claimed that the drug could lower a person's ego defenses and make him unable to lie. I had observed the fleeting and curiously unrepeatable clearing of catatonic schizophrenia during an Amytal interview, so the truth serum idea did not seem altogether implausible to me.

The procedure was simple enough. No one considered issues of informed consent in those days, so the patient was simply told to lie down on a bed for a treatment. An attempt was made to get the patient as relaxed and as comfortable as possible. A syringe was filled with the barbiturate solution and the needle of the syringe was introduced into a vein, usually at the bend of the elbow known as the anticubital fossa. The patient was then asked to count backwards while the drug was slowly injected. When the patient's voice became slurred, the injection was stopped and the interview was begun, with additional doses of the drug given if the patient seemed to be becoming too alert.

It was quite some time before I found what seemed to me a proper candidate for an Amytal interview, other than mute catatonic schizophrenics who were sometimes able to talk under Amytal sedation. One snowy winter day, the police brought in a man who had been caught shoplifting an overcoat from a clothing store. He was a local man who lived on a small military pension, and was known to be a heavy drinker. He had not appeared to be intoxicated when the police arrested him, but he claimed to have no memory of the shoplifting episode.

To me, he seemed to be a candidate for truth serum. Was he just lying, or had something happened to induce some sort of a fugue state? In a fugue state, an individual may act in uncharacteristic ways and afterwards have no memory for the event, but the memories may sometimes be recovered during an Amytal interview.

A student nurse saw me gathering the materials I needed for the procedure and asked me what I was going to do. When I told her, she asked if she could watch. I told her I would be happy to have her assistance. So the nurse, the patient, and I found a quiet room and began. I told the patient to relax with his eyes closed and to start counting backwards from 100. He began counting and I began the injection. As is the case with alcoholics, he had a high tolerance for the sedative, and his count was almost down to 50 before there was any slurring of his speech. At that point I stopped injecting the Amytal and asked him to imagine he was back in time just before he walked into the department store where he was arrested.

The patient seemed to have a hard time talking, and I will not try to imitate his intoxicated-sounding speech, but he gave us the following story:

"You see, it was like this. I was standing on the street corner last Friday when this beautiful blond lady in a yellow Cadillac convertible pulls up and says, 'Want a ride, fellow?'

"I say, 'Why not?' and hop in with her. So we drive a long way around country roads I could never find again till we come to this mansion. We go in and it's the most wonderful place you ever saw. There is even an indoor swimming pool. She points to a little door off the pool and says for me to change into a bathing suit so I can swim with her.

Well, she changes and so do I. Then we swim a little. Then we take off our bathing suits and make love. Then we put our suits back on and a servant brings a great meal with wine. And so it was till Monday morning, nothing but swimming, eating, drinking, and making love. On Monday morning she tells me to put on my own clothes and she drives me back to where she picked me up. Then she kisses me and disappears."

The nurse was giving me an incredulous look, and I explained, "You have just heard 'The Yellow Convertible Lie.' Servicemen returning from weekend leave often told some version of that story. I suspect the Jungians would say it's a part of the male collective unconscious, and that God or evolution put it there for the protection of males who return after a fruitless search for a mate...Let's try again with a little more drug."

I had him count down again and gave him enough of the drug to stop his counting. He seemed asleep and gave a little snore, so I shook him gently, suggested strongly that this time he would have to tell the truth. Again we listened. Now he was almost unintelligible but he still managed to spin another implausible yarn. This time he said a lawyer had come up to him and told him that an old man for whom he used to work had died and left him a fortune. He was embroidering on that story when he seemed to slip off to sleep.

I looked at the nurse and said, "Well, so much for truth serum!" Then, as I was putting a gauze patch over the needle in preparation for taking it out of his vein, the patient roused himself and said, "Hey, Doc, what about another little shot of that stuff before you quit?"

Of course, pharmacologically, there is no reason that Amytal would incline one to veracity more than would alcohol. And although the old Romans said *in vino veritas*, what modern anthropologist would consider talking with a drunk in order to learn what life is really like for an alcoholic?

16

The Pet Paranoid

Our nervous systems are attuned to change, and except in certain cases of pathological pains, they stop responding to an unchanging stimulus. By the same token, a smoothly running routine tends to be overlooked, but if anything goes wrong, we start casting about for someone to blame. Thus it is natural for public institutions to be generally ignored when they function well, but if there is any trouble, they get attacked promptly by members of the public. While some of those attacks are uncalled for, unfortunately some are justified. If justified attacks on institutions could be matched with efforts to correct the faults, it would be a better world.

There are certain people who specialize in attacking institutions and in finding fault, but who have surprisingly little interest in getting involved with corrective action. Some such people are so unusually suspicious that they can be said to have paranoid personalities. Their thought processes are well enough organized so that they cannot be labeled psychotic, but they see conspiracies when none exist and tend to lack the social contacts that might mitigate their misperceptions. Feedback from our friends is a big factor in keeping our ideas from straying too far afield, and is referred to as consensual validation in "psycho-speak." The combination of intelligence, a suspicious nature, and relative social isolation seems to contribute to the development of paranoid personalities, and some of them are particularly difficult to deal with.

From time to time such individuals make demands for change that are not well founded, and on occasion they can be pretty destructive. Around 1948, there was a lawyer in Worcester who decided that the hospital was keeping people locked up for evil reasons, and he decided to attack the unscrupulous, devious physicians who were behind the sinister cabal.

Most of the time Dr. Bardwell Flower, our superintendent, seemed to be so occupied with his administrative problems that he left Dr. Rothschild pretty much alone. Although they had offices across the lobby from each other, they did not appear to meet often. However, one morning, as I was on my way to the front of the hospital, I saw Rothschild leaving the superintendent's office with a look of intense concentration on his face. Gurrey, switchboard operator and purveyor of hot gossip, told us that some lawyer was raising hell with Flower, and that Flower had passed the ball to Rothschild. It seemed that an ex-patient had filled the lawyer's ear with horror stories about the hospital but refused to let the lawyer reveal the complainant's name.

About two days later we were surprised to find a rather formally attired stranger sitting among us at a staff meeting. He was a relatively big man, but the only unusual thing I remember was that he wore dark glasses, which he replaced by clear pince-nez glasses when he was reading charts. When Rothschild came in, he introduced the stranger as Mr. Goldman, a lawyer, and said we should be as helpful as possible in trying to meet Mr. Goldman's requests. We were also told that Mr. Goldman had been cleared by the Department of Mental Health in Boston to have access to confidential patient files and had their permission to interview any patient at any time he chose.

Later, in Goldman's absence, Rothschild told us the story of Goldman's interest in the state hospital and confided that he hoped to show Goldman something of the problems we faced. That way, he hoped that Goldman would use his crusading energies on behalf of the hospital. I guess that in spite of Rothschild's clinical acumen, he did not know how rare it is to get constructive work out of a critical crusader.

During the following week, we saw Mr. Goldman on the wards for an hour or so almost every day. To the staff he was cordial but formal. Most of the time he appeared to be carefully screening the patients on the more acute wards for someone who would complain of mistreatment or wrongful incarceration.

Now, in those days, simply being judged to be a public nuisance was enough to get you into the hospital, so I was sure he would find someone to confirm his suspicions. Sure enough, before long he began to spend most of his time with Roger Fitch, and I reported this to Rothschild.

Roger was one of those people that fall through the cracks in the standard Diagnostic and Statistical Nomenclature. He was not truly schizophrenic, as he lacked the formal thought disorder. He was suspicious to the point of paranoia, but there was no bizarre organized delusional system. He had the superficial manipulative charm of a psychopathic personality. He was an episodic alcoholic. He certainly had an impulse disorder, for he had episodes of destructive rages. There was also a bipolar flavor to his behavior, for self-condemnation and suicidal depression could follow his rages. To top it all off he was a liar and a thief.

He was in one of his better periods when he met Mr. Goldman, and they hit it off famously. Roger could be really charming, and soon Goldman was convinced that we were mistreating Roger by keeping him in the hospital. So Goldman lodged a formal complaint with Rothschild demanding that Roger be released.

Rothschild was facing increasing pressure to discharge more patients, so he agreed to send Roger out on a trial visit if Goldman would take him into his home and vouch for his behavior. Rothschild suggested that it would be wise for Goldman to learn more about why Roger was hospitalized, but Goldman was uninterested. I still wonder how much the discharge of Roger had to do with the nascent idea that discharge was good in itself over and above any concern for the individual patient's welfare.

A few days later we learned that Goldman had crossed Roger and evoked one of Roger's rages. Goldman had left his house in fear, and returned to find Roger gone along with a bedside clock and a modest sum of money that had been on Goldman's bedside table.

I wish I could report that Goldman came to recognize that we were doing our best and so ended up as a staunch supporter of the hospital. But paranoia is the ultimate ego trip. Goldman accused Rothschild of setting him up, and after that we heard no more from Goldman. I assume he found some other arena where he was more successful in confirming his belief that evil surrounded him, and where he could, by the contrast, reassure himself of his own virtue.

17

The Patient Who Smelled Like a Darkroom

Worcester State Hospital had a hospital within a hospital. Patients with physical illnesses who posed management problems beyond the capabilities of Memorial Hospital, the general hospital in town, were admitted to our medical services. We had a staff internist and a staff surgeon. The internist was Dr. Werner Jaffee. His wife, a gentile German physician, had saved him from the Holocaust in the late 1930s. He was a fast study. He had his United States license, spoke English without an accent, and even told jokes in English! His wife retained a thick accent, did not practice, and bemoaned the fact that she was no longer addressed as *Frau Doktor Doktor*.

I do not remember the surgeon's name, but she was a handsome woman who was always elegantly dressed. I do, however, remember clearly that she wore high heels in the operating room, which she explained was to underline the fact that she could be feminine and a surgeon at the same time.

As a consequence of our having this backup hospital, we saw a wide variety of psychoses secondary to physical illnesses, and had a number of rare "museum pieces" on the chronic services. There were a few post-encephalitic Parkinson patients of the sort that Oliver Sacks described so well in his book, *Awakenings*. They usually stood immobilized except for the constant "pill-rolling" tremor of their hands. One Parkinson patient played catcher on the softball team. He would stand behind the plate, immobile except for the tremor until the ball came speeding towards his head. Then, in response to the external stimulus of the pitched ball, he would galvanize into action, make the appropriate play and then lapse back into his former state.

One patient had Wilson's disease, a rare defect in copper metabolism that causes a greenish ring around the pupil, mental retardation, and bizarre movements of the arms and shoulders called wing beating.

Neurological symptoms were usually given German names in those days, so wing-beating was known as *fleugelspangen*. These days, if Wilson's disease is caught early, it can be treated with chelating agents that remove the excess copper from the patient's system.

Several patients had Huntington's disease. That tragic congenital disorder is best known to the lay public because it killed Woody Guthrie, and will, I hope, soon vanish beneath the onslaught of modern molecular biology. Unfortunately, now as in those days, depression, dementia, dance-like movements known as chorea, and a writhing known as athetosis mark its terminal stage. These assorted movement disorders added a particularly bizarre quality to our back wards.

It was before the era of recreational drugs, so we did not see many of the toxic states that come into emergency rooms nowadays, but we had our own collection of toxic states. We saw some methyl (wood) alcohol intoxication, a few methamphetamine overdoses, quite a few cases of delirium tremens, and an occasional really odd patient. One such patient was a case of bromism.

In days gone by, bromides were used much as minor tranquilizers are used today. Boring tales were called "bromides" because they put one to sleep. In 1950, the BromoSeltzer tower was still a landmark in Baltimore. I do not know just when bromide sedatives went out of fashion, but I rather suspect they were superceded by barbiturates somewhere around 1940.

One day, a patient came in who was clearly in some sort of a toxic delirium. I admitted him to the medical service and was completing my workup when Jaffee, our internist, walked in. I called him over and said, "There's something strange going on here. His family claims that he did not have any prior illness, does not drink, and does not take any medicines that they know of, but he looks toxic to me. Furthermore, he smells like a photographic darkroom."

Jaffee came over, checked the patient, and sniffed his breath. Then he said, "I'm going to show you some magic."

He had me restrain the patient and get some intravenous fluids started. While I was finishing up, he returned with a nasogastric tube, a syringe with some histamine in it, and an emesis basin. He gave the patient the histamine, then passed the tube through his nose into his stomach, and began aspirating stomach contents.

To my amazement, the fluid that he withdrew from the patient's stomach was violet-colored and had the unmistakable odor of hydrobromic acid. Jaffee explained, "The stomach will put out hydrobromic acid in preference to hydrochloric acid when there is appreciable bromine in the blood stream. The histamine stimulates gastric acid secretion, and we are now replacing his bromide ions with chloride ions."

Before my very eyes, the patient began to come out of his delirium and by the time the stomach contents were colorless, he was quite normal and cooperative. It seems our patient had a box full of BromoSeltzer that was some 10 or more years old. He had been using it from time to time as sort of a tranquilizer when he got upset. Now of course bromine is an element and does not loose its potency with time, but our patient did not know that, and decided to up his usual dose since the pills had been sitting around so long. He reacted with a mild confusion. Then, the more disturbed he got, the more BromoSeltzer he took, until he was in a full-blown delirium.

In those days, among the medical upper crust, showing off was a perfectly acceptable way of getting approval. When I was a medical intern at Grady Hospital, morning rounds with Dr. Paul Beeson were no-holds-barred competitions with house staff trying to impress Beeson and Beeson equally fiercely trying (and usually succeeding) to overawe the house staff. I was impressed by Jaffee making an obscure diagnosis by the smell of a patient's breath, and so I fantasized about a time in the future when I could awe my colleagues by diagnosing bromism from a distance. Not only have I never seen another case of bromism, but I also learned that, except in rare academic environments (Paul Beeson's rounds at Grady Hospital and the Worcester staff dining room being the only examples that come to mind), being a smart-ass show off was not the way to win friends and influence people.

18

Psychiatry, the Cinderella of Medicine, before the Fairy Godmother (aka the Pharmaceutical Industry) Found Glass Slippers for Her Feet

Cinderella seems an apt metaphor for psychiatry in 1948. Medicine and surgery were getting glorious new synthetic drugs while stepsister psychiatry had to make do with some pretty odd stuff. The other metaphor that comes to mind is the Donner party, whose members starved to death on the banks of the Truckee River, which was full of trout. Like the unfortunate Donner party, we were ignorant of the traditional or native resources that were all around us.

In the 1930s, the Drug Enforcement Administration and the Treasury Department had joined forces to criminalize herbal products. At that time, confronted by the repeal of Prohibition, Harry J. Anslinger, Commissioner of Narcotics, Bureau of Narcotics, Department of the Treasury, saved his superb alcohol control police from unemployment by turning marijuana from a weed, used in the barrios and by jazz musicians, into the "Devil Drug." Dr. Carl Bowman, then Professor of Psychiatry at University of California San Francisco, led a losing fight against that absurdity.

Alcohol and tobacco were legal and protected by powerful lobbies. Marijuana was criminalized. Yet we now know that, of all the intoxicating substances, marijuana has rather minimal associated adverse effects. It is the least addicting, has minor withdrawal effects, and produces little long-term damage except in heavy users. Not to say that it does not dumb one down, and really heavy users can experience withdrawal effects, but people intoxicated with marijuana are almost never involved in violence.

The federal drug police did do some good, although in the long run their record is not wonderful. For example, they got the cocaine out of soft drinks, which was useful socially, but since then they have managed to elevate the cocaine trade to levels of evil, violence, and sophistication never dreamed of by alcohol bootleggers. In passing, I cannot help recollecting the cocaine bottles at Worcester that always stood ready on the trays for minor eye, nose, and throat procedures.

They also cracked down on the Native American Church and its use of peyote. The traditional use of the mescaline-containing peyote cactus buttons by American Indians in their religious ceremonies could hardly be seen as any kind of a public health problem, and in fact it was associated with reduced alcoholism among the users. Of course, if I were a drug enforcement agent, I'd rather bust pueblo Indians and jazz musicians than shoot it out with coke dealers.

But the end result was that, in 1948, drugs derived from plants, including those derived from cocoa leaves and poppy sap, were mostly illegal, and I had never heard of other herbal medications except for those that had yielded synthetic drugs. I do not think I ever heard of Valerian or St. John's Wort until the 1960s, and somehow (thanks to the tobacco companies) we never thought of tobacco as a psychoactive drug.

Not only did the Drug Enforcement Administration inhibit interest in herbal products, but on top of that, synthetic drugs were revolutionizing medicine and surgery. The sulfonamides had already revolutionized the treatment of infectious diseases, and penicillin was truly a miracle drug, literally eradicating central nervous system syphilis and turning dermatologists (who used to make their livings treating syphilis) into oncologists who treated skin cancers. With the exception of penicillin (for syphilis), psychiatrists were yet to get much help from the chemists, but we never thought to look at native remedies.

Around 1930, barbiturates had replaced the bromides that had been introduced around the turn of the century, but there were still a lot of weird sedatives around. Psychiatrists had chloral hydrate, which is a real survivor. It was introduced in the first decade of the twentieth century and is still around today. Its lasting fame rests in its having been the active ingredient of the infamous Mickey Finn of San Francisco's Barbary Coast. That part of town was called the Barbary Coast because of its similarity to the lawless coast in North Africa that was home to some particularly bloodthirsty pirates. Much the same area in modern San Francisco is called North Beach, and it still has its share of bars.

Being potent and almost tasteless, an anesthetic dose of chloral hydrate added to rotgut whisky could go undetected. When a healthy-looking young man entered a participating bar, the bartender would "slip him a Mickey." When the unfortunate victim of the Mickey Finn woke up, he was usually on a ship headed for the Orient, hence the term Shanghaied.

Then there was a drug called Avertin, which was given by enema when vomiting was a risk or when the patient refused oral medication. Unfortunately, the sedative dose was not far from the dose that stopped the patient from breathing.

Barbiturates were recognized as dangerous, particularly when used to treat psychotic patients. There were paradoxical reactions, where the patient would become more and more excited as the dose was increased up to the point of respiratory and cardiac arrest. Sometimes scopolamine would produce a curious calming, although it induces delirium in normal subjects. However, it was not particularly safe, as it could lead to fatal hyperthermia (overheating).

But the most memorable of all those antique sedatives was paraldehyde. It is no longer listed in the *Physicians Desk Reference*, but the Drug Enforcement Administration still lists it as an approved drug for inpatient treatment of delirium tremens (the sometimes-fatal reaction to alcohol withdrawal associated with hallucinations and seizures). Paraldehyde was safe, efficacious, and could be given by mouth or intramuscularly. Usually, after one intramuscular injection the patient would cooperate and take an oral dose, because paraldehyde produced moderate pain at the site of injection. Now, I hasten to add that this was not torture disguised as "Behavior Modification." Rather, when we had a wildly agitated case of delirium tremens, sedation was a life-saving measure. A struggling patient could aspirate the drug, and that was not good for the lungs to say the least. So if there was more cooperation when the second dose was offered orally, all the better.

Paraldehyde had another advantage. The lungs excreted it, so patients with renal and liver problems were not so vulnerable to a toxic buildup. It was the drug of choice when we had a newly admitted delirious patient suffering from alcohol withdrawal whose yellow eyeballs and enlarged knobby liver suggested that he had not much hepatic function left over to metabolize any other drug. I can remember the magical and lifesaving tranquilization of a particular 200-pound drunk who was seriously ill both physically and mentally. Within minutes after the paraldehyde, we were able to loosen his restraints and get intravenous fluids started. It was not only fast-acting but also long-acting, with a good dose effective for up to 24 hours.

But the virtue of pulmonary excretion for the patient was vice for staff. The stuff stank, and the patient who had been given a dose could smell up the whole ward while his lungs disposed of the drug. In doing research for this book, I learned, to my surprise, that the Drug Enforcement Administration still warns of paraldehyde addiction, adding that some people prefer it to alcohol in spite of the smell. But of course, there are some people who will abuse anything. In the 1960s, when benzodiazepines like Valium (diazepam) were introduced, paraldehyde was quickly relegated to category of rarely used agents, and survives mainly in the vivid olfactory memories of those of us who lived through the times when we had nothing better.

19

Never Say Die

Worcester residents were not rushing from one hospital to the next for special rotations, as was the case in some of the university-based residencies. Living in the hospital with our patients, we were able to follow our patients over time. Even when we moved from one service in the hospital to the next, we still ran into our old patients and heard about their lives from our colleagues. This gave us the opportunity, educational and sometimes humbling, of seeing our predictions tested by the passage of time. This next story is about the virtue of following up one's prognostications, although in this case my education was delivered fairly quickly.

Mr. O'Malley was about 70 years old, and in the eyes of a young, 25-year-old resident like me, he had already lived longer than was his due. O'Malley had been admitted to the general hospital in Worcester with the diagnosis of left sided cerebrovascular accident. He was quickly transferred to The Worcester State Hospital medical service because of confused and agitated behavior that was hard to manage. Mr. O'Malley weighed over 200 pounds, and in spite of his age he had a good physique. Thus, even with a spastic paralysis of his right arm and leg (right hemiplegia) and an inability to speak (aphasia), he was a handful when he began to thrash around.

O'Malley had more relatives coming to visit him than was usually the case with state hospital patients, but in his confused and aphasic state, he did not seem to recognize any of them. I soon learned that Mr. O'Malley was moderately wealthy and the head of a large clan. The visitors, who turned out to be siblings and offspring, seemed overly solicitous. They also seemed particularly anxious for me to give them a prognosis.

I had previously taken care of another patient who I thought had been quite similar to Mr. O'Malley at the start of his illness. Over several months this earlier patient had suffered additional strokes and now was on a back ward with severe multi-infarct dementia. That unfortunate man was likely to continue having strokes, and to remain demented until a last stroke ended his life. So, after about a week and without consulting my betters, I delivered my doleful prognosis to the assembled family members. "Mr. O'Malley," I said, "will probably not recover. Rather, I expect him to have more strokes and to become even more disabled, both physically and mentally."

The family took my news with much lighter spirits than I had expected. As they departed, one of my patient's children remarked to me that the old man was a tightfisted tyrant and that the family would be all too willing to take over his financial responsibilities. I had not exactly expected that reaction, but I figured it was all for the best.

However, over the next few days, Mr. O'Malley began an entirely unexpected and remarkable recovery. His aphasia cleared, and with the return of the ability to talk, his confusion and agitation disappeared. While the hordes of relatives had vanished after my prognostic pronouncement, O'Malley still had one constant visitor. She was an attractive younger woman who, I learned, was Mr. O'Malley's mistress. She often helped the nurses feed him, and was clearly overjoyed when he began to regain the use of his spastic right arm.

As Mr. O'Malley continued with his remarkable recovery, he was able to tell me that he had been aware of his crowd of visitors and wondered what had become of them. Sheepishly, I confessed that they had vanished after I had made my obviously erroneous prediction about his inevitable downhill course.

"Great God Almighty!" said O'Malley. Turning to his young girlfriend, he said, "Sally, call Bill Kelly and tell him to hotfoot it over here. We've got damage control to do." Then turning to me again he asked, "Any place private where I could talk to my lawyer when he gets here?" Embarrassed, I felt the least I could do was to offer him my office for an hour.

The next day, we discharged the patient and I never saw anything of the O'Malley clan again. But some time later I heard through the grapevine about the consequences of my defective clinical judgment. Mr. O'Malley's family had rushed to have him declared incompetent and had been in the process of establishing a conservatorship for his financial holdings. On discovering what was afoot, my ex-patient had disinherited the bunch and married his mistress, Sally. According to my informant, Sally and Mr. O'Malley were blissfully happy.

I felt guilty about my role in getting the family disinherited and destroying O'Malley's relationships with his kin. I wished I had asked some advice before shooting off my mouth. However, supervision was a sometime thing at Worcester, and because of my experience with the prior patient, it never occurred to me I could be so far off base. At any rate, ever since Mr. O'Malley, I have been much more circumspect about foretelling the future.

Since O'Malley, I have pretty much given up trying to play medical Nostradamus. On the other hand, thanks to new drugs, to new psycho-therapeutic techniques, and I hope to more than 50 years of experience, my luck as a therapist is much improved.

20

Folie À Deux

When two or more people share a delusional system, it is referred to as a *folie à deux* (for two people) or *à trois* (for three). When the crowd gets larger, there is no formal diagnostic label, although I suppose these bigger groups can pass as cults, religions, or even political parties. Most of the cases I have seen as a psychiatrist were relatively classic *folie à deux*. It begins with two people living together and having little contact with the rest of the world. One is relatively normal to begin with, while the other is floridly psychotic. Little by little the psychotic member of the duo bullies the other into accepting his or her delusional system. I have read of occasions when such madness expands to become a sort of communal psychosis. With the case of Mr. and Mrs. Thornton, the delusional system (if you want to call it that) was truly shared and mutual.

The Thorntons were a sweet little old New England couple in their eighties, gray-headed and rather shrunken-looking, as osteoporosis was not treated in those days. I inherited the couple when I was on the outpatient after-care service, so I do not really recall their admissions to the hospital. However, from their records, I knew that they had been brought in by the Secret Service and housed initially on the maximum-security units.

The Thorntons had lived in a cottage that fronted on the village green of a small Massachusetts town. Mrs. Thornton's mother had lived there all her life, and some 40 years ago the couple had moved in to care for her. The mother was now dead, and the Thorntons had no children and no close relations, so they lived more or less isolated lives.

The town where they lived was withering on the vine, so the local movers and shakers had decided that the village green would be a great place for a shopping mall. The Thorntons objected. I was never clear about exactly what followed. It seemed there was something in the town charter that made converting the green to a shopping center a bit of a problem so long as the Thorntons objected. There also seemed to have been some threats, veiled or otherwise, made to the Thorntons, hinting that powerful political figures would not take it kindly if the Thorntons stood in the way of progress.

At his wife's urging, Mr. Thornton wrote letters to the local paper but they were ignored. He wrote to local legislators, then to his congressman and his senators. Nothing happened. Then he decided that the President of the United States had to be behind the evil cabal, so Mr. Thornton wrote a letter to the President. The Secret Service proceeded to investigate the Thorntons whom they perceived as a threat to the President.

After their first month in the hospital, the Secret Service seemed to have lost interest in them, and I was told the Thorntons could be discharged if they would not write any more letters to the President. I spent some time listening to them, and quite frankly thought there was more reality in their delusional system than is usually the case. However, the Thorntons and I came to the consensus that there is a point where fighting city hall becomes unproductive. So between the three of us and the Secret Service, discharge was approved contingent on six monthly visits with me.

Under instructions from Rothschild, I simply listened and carefully avoided checking out any of the details that they related, so I could honestly say that I had no reason to doubt their story. I told them to tell me anything they wanted to, and promised it would go no further if they so desired. However, I emphasized that they should not write any more letters to the President, for if they did, they would be right back in the hospital.

For the next six months we had a cordial relationship, but their belief in a plot against them directed by the President of the United States remained shared, unshaken, and kept secret between the three of us. As to the shopping mall, I left Worcester before it was started, but I suspect the Thorntons lost out in the end.

I have no doubt that society was treating the Thorntons unfairly. In most cases of delusions, one can make the diagnosis because of disorders in the patient's thought processes. For example, in the case of paranoid schizophrenics, the police may indeed be keeping an eye on them. So the diagnosis of a paranoid delusion does not require that the delusion be false. The Thorntons had nothing abnormal about their thought processes, and that was not the only time that I felt social actions would do more good for my patients than my psychiatric skills. I am sure that the impotence I feel when I find that apparent psychopathology is actually the result of evil in society is shared by most of my colleagues in the healing professions.

21

My Nose Receives a Silver Rod at Harvard

Within the medical community, a certain ambivalence toward the medical school at Harvard University is relatively common. This is in part because some graduates from both Harvard Medical School and the undergraduate school adopt superior attitudes. I remember when I was a boy in a small southern town, the older brother of my then girlfriend went off to Harvard. When he returned, the general consensus was that Harvard had turned a perfectly fine young man into an arrogant obnoxious ass. When I was attending Columbia College from 1941 to 1943, both Columbians and Harvard people tacitly agreed that Harvard was a cut above Columbia on the social scale, if not in measures of scholastic excellence.

When, in 1951, I came to work at the University of California San Francisco, I was impressed by the fact that UCSF had produced more Nobel laureates and had more federal research funding than had Harvard Medical School. However, the New England Journal of Medicine and Harvard's public relations machine made it seem that Harvard Medical School and its teaching hospital, Massachusetts General Hospital, represented medicine at its best, a sort of perfection that other institutions could only unsuccessfully try to emulate. Later, in his 1978 book, *The House of God*, Samuel Shem[4] poked wonderful fun at the Harvard Medical School hubris. The "House of God" was of course Massachusetts General. "Mount St. Elsewhere" was the "inferior" community hospital where they sent uninteresting patients. "Mount St. Elsewhere" was later the title of a TV series. Shem coined many wonderful acronyms, as for example GOOMER, for difficult but uninteresting patients. Spelled out, it is "Get out of my emergency room."

On the other hand, I can testify that some people who go to Harvard undergraduate school can remain lovely human beings because, at the Columbia College of Physicians and Surgeons, two of my best friends and roommates were from Harvard. This note of course echoes the cliché of the prejudiced: "Some of my best friends are [fill in the blank]."

All of this is by way of explaining my ambivalent feelings when Hoagland sent me to visit Harvard. I was aware of the EEG work being done at Harvard by Jacob Feinsinger, Mary A.B. Brazier, and Paul MacLean. Later, I would go with Feinsinger to start the Department of Psychiatry at the University of Maryland, School of Medicine. Hoagland decided that, at Worcester, we should use special leads for EEG recording that could be passed up the nose to rest near the base of the brain. These were called nasopharangeal leads, and Hoagland said I should go to Brazier and MacLean at Massachusetts General Hospital for instruction in the technique. I was both excited and intimidated. I have always been, if anything, a little too fond of novel experiences, but on the other hand I have never liked being put in a situation where people could act superior and be condescending.

Nasopharangeal leads were important because they allowed one to make electrical contact with the nasopharynx, a place where the inside of the nose and the base of the skull come close together. What you can record of the brain's electrical activity depends on where the electrodes are located. The nearer you are to the locus of some abnormal activity, the better, but, except for recordings associated with neurosurgery, the electrodes must be placed outside the skull.

The temporal lobes of the brain are folded under so that they lie just above the bones at the roof of the nose. That means they are at some distance from any place on the scalp or face. So nasopharangeal leads were of interest because they allowed one to get an electrode close to the temporal lobes without surgery.

The temporal lobes are particularly interesting because epileptic seizures in them are often associated with abnormal behavior. The behavior is most often benign, like staring into space, sniffing, and tapping fingers. There is still a lively controversy around the relationship between temporal epilepsy and violent or antisocial behavior. Some neuroscientists will testify in court that some piece of violent antisocial behavior was the result of temporal lobe epilepsy, while others will claim that temporal lobe epileptics are no more or less liable to be violent than anyone else. That is not my fight, but if I had to bet, I would put my money on the ones who claim that epileptics are not particularly likely to be violent or criminal.

Hoagland had seen some of MacLean's recordings and wanted to see if we could repeat them. So nothing would do but for me to call and arrange for a demonstration and a lesson in the use of the nasopharangeal electrodes. I called a number that Hoagland had given me and was greeted by a charming, well-bred, British, female voice. That was my first, but by no means my last, contact with Dr. Mary A.B. Brazier, better known as

"Molly" to three generations of electroencephalographers. She suggested a time when Paul MacLean would be on hand, and when I agreed, she continued with directions.

"Come to the old medical school building and ask anyone for the ether dome. You'll find us tucked under the amphitheater seats on the left."

I dutifully set out for Boston, where I knew driving conditions were more like those on *Insurgentes* in Mexico City or around the *Étoile* in Paris than like anything elsewhere in the United States. However, following Molly's helpful directions, I evaded the aggressive and somewhat irrational Boston motorists and soon found myself in the ether dome. I was truly awed. Looking down into the amphitheater, I could visualize Morton giving his demonstration of di-ethyl ether as a general anesthetic, just as the event is memorialized in the well-known, heroic, and inaccurate painting by Robert Hinkley. Having interned at Grady Hospital in Atlanta, I was also familiar with the fact that Dr. Crawford W. Long had used ether anesthesia in Georgia some years before Morton, the dentist-entrepreneur, introduced it in Massachusetts. True to form, Harvard claimed priority of discovery.

A voice from beneath the seats of the amphitheater called out, "Down here!" I went down to the floor and around to the side where I discovered a small EEG cage, a Grass electroencephalograph like the one we had at Worcester, and two people in white coats who introduced themselves as Molly Brazier and Paul MacLean. Molly was an attractive blond with the irregular teeth that I associate with the British upper middle class of the era. Paul was a spare man with a bow tie, which seemed to be his lifelong sartorial signature.

From a bottle of sterilizing solution, Paul produced a round silver rod about one-fourth of an inch in diameter and about five inches long. It had been bent into a sort of s-shape. There was a slight bulb on one end and a wire on the other.

"Here's the beast," Paul said. "Now, the best way to learn how to insert it is for me to put it up your nose once and then have you put it up your own nose. By doing it to yourself, you really get the feel of it. After that, you should have no trouble repeating the process when you get back to Worcester." As usual, I was up for anything new.

While Molly was turning on the EEG machine, Paul picked up an atomizer bottle from the instrument table and told me, "Squirt a little of this cocaine up your preferred nostril. I can do it to myself without anesthetic, but to start with, it's a good idea to numb the nose a little." In those days, cocaine was the topical anesthetic of choice for eye, nose, and throat procedures, and supplies of the drug routinely stood unguarded on setup trays.

Then Molly came over with three surface electrodes, and I sat still while she put electrodes on both ears and the vertex of my scalp. Then I sprayed the inside of my right nostril with cocaine. When I felt my nose become a little numb, I sat back in the chair used for EEG recording. Paul picked up a piece of paper and in a matter of fact voice diagrammed the placement of the electrode. "The shaft has a thin coat of shellac so you have to get the tip against the top of the nasopharynx for a good contact."

I leaned back and, slick as a whistle, Paul slipped the thing up my nose. Molly read off the inter-electrode resistances and commented, "Nice contact."

Next I heard the familiar scratching of the EEG pens, and then the sound of Molly tearing off a piece of record. The three of us together looked at the strip of paper with its squiggly ink lines. It was nice clean recording with my usual booming alpha rhythm coming through on all leads and no 60 cycle noise.

"Well, I see you're not a genius," Paul remarked as he examined the record.

I looked puzzled and Molly chimed in, "Norbert Weiner has no alpha and says that's because he's a genius. Geniuses use all their brain all the time while awake and so always have their alpha suppressed." Weiner was the genius behind the guidance systems that had made our guns so formidable in WWII.[5]

I must have looked a little crestfallen because Paul added, "Molly and I have lots of alpha, too, so we're all in the same boat."

Then, as directed, I practiced on myself a few times. I eventually got the hang of sliding the thing all the way up my nose so as to produce a clean recording.

Paul took the electrode from me, wrapped it in cotton, put it in a box and handed it to me.

"Gee, thanks!" I said (or something equally banal).

"Had it made especially for you guys to use at Worcester and you are welcome!" said Molly.

And so I departed from Harvard with about 20 ounces of silver, a numb right nostril, and some warm memories. As I drove back towards Worcester, I thought to myself that I was glad to be more like Molly Brazier and Paul MacLean than like Norbert Weiner, although I suppose I would have traded a little of my alpha activity for a little more intelligence.

Part 2

Doctor, Please Make the Voices Go Away

22

A Special Place

Living with madness had a few perks for the supposedly sane. In the second year of my residency training, my wife and I were awarded a grand room in the state hospital on the second floor of the administration building. It was known as the "Bridal Suite" because it had been decorated when superintendent Quimby got married around 1910. It had faded cabbage rose wallpaper, a marble bathroom, a pull-chain toilet, and a huge tub that stood on claw-foot legs. It also adjoined one of the conference rooms, which gave us occasional privileged insights into the hospital operations.

Senior staff went home to their houses for lunch and dinner, but junior staff who lived in the hospital ate almost all their meals in the staff dining room. Many of the staff who lived outside also ate their lunches there. All meals were served from the common kitchen, where meals for the patients were prepared. One day, my wife Dorothy overheard a meeting of superintendents from all of the Massachusetts State hospitals, because it was being held in the conference room next to our bedroom. They were discussing how much oatmeal could be added to ground meat in the making of meat loaf. Dorothy was not surprised at some of the meat/oatmeal ratios she heard proposed. Indeed, one of our more witty colleagues had suggested that the meat loaf might be improved by scraping off the soupy tomato sauce and adding brown sugar and milk.

The food was laughably unpalatable, but that was the worst of it. As bad as the rest of Worcester State Hospital may seem from the twenty-first century, and at the risk of being repetitive, the Worcester State Hospital at mid-twentieth century was not the run-of-the-mill state hospital. First, it was awash with students. We had neurology residents and medical students. We had trainees in nursing, psychology, occupational therapy, and social work. Most of the assorted trainees came from Clark University, Boston University, and Tufts. I think Boston Psychopathic, now known as Massachusetts Mental Health Center, must have taken care of the Harvard students, as we never saw any of them. Having swarms of students looking over everyone's shoulder

The cast of characters. The second year house staff and faculty (? indicates that I cannot remember the name). From left to right, back row standing: Vangebedian, Cullinan, Banay, ?, Houseman, Currier, ?. Second row sitting: Hoagland, Sands, Flower, Rothchild, Jaffee. Front row sitting or crouching on the ground: Morarty, Simonson, Modell, Teplin, The Surgeon (I cannot remember her name), Author, ?

contributes to the quality of patient care even if it is not cost-effective, and is in general a stimulus both to more rational staff behavior and to ethical administrative decisions.

Perhaps it is even more significant that most of us at Worcester were truly residents. In the usual hospital, the term "medical resident" is an anachronism, a reference to the live-in arrangements for young doctors that are a casualty of the better pay and working conditions enjoyed by today's resident physicians. Given the relative isolation of Worcester State and the resident's minute housing allowance, as soon as someone moved out and in-hospital housing became available, the next resident took it. So, Worcester State became a sort of a co-ed monastery/convent, with keys instead of crosses and white coats instead of woolen habits. That metaphor can be pushed even further as we shared a religion-like goal: to help those who suffered from mental illness. All of these factors fostered a great camaraderie.

For us residents, the intellectual atmosphere was particularly stimulating. This was in part a function of the interaction between the Worcester State Hospital and the Worcester Foundation for Experimental Biology. Between the hospital programs and the foundation programs, we were exposed to outstanding experts on everything from Information Sciences such as Cybernetics to metaphysics such as Psychoanalysis. Some experts were on the staff of the hospital or the foundation, some scientists came to speak at the once-a-month hospital/foundation seminars, and some clinicians from the hinterlands "West of the Hudson River" stayed at the hospital for several days. Behind this all was the faith that some overarching science would emerge from a synthesis of the disparate disciplines and give us a basic science of human behavior. Among today's scientists, the consensus is that Nature has no grand plan, but simply tinkers. Maybe so, but I still long for the elegance of my lost faith.

But back to my assertion that Worcester State Hospital was a special place. To further illustrate that point, I will tell the story of Dave Moriarity. Dave was a good, compassionate, and enthusiastic young physician, and I hope I am not being self-congratulatory in saying he was much like the rest of us. I also need to emphasize our youth. During WWII, we had all been hurried through college and medical school so we could be used as medical officers in the war. The result was that, as a group, we had reached our residencies with both more immaturity and more energy than is usually the case. We worked 12-hour days, but we had night duty only one night in four and weekend duty only once a month. That was a piece of cake after the 72 hours on and 24 hours off we had worked during our internships. While I never had the feeling that lack of money prevented us from doing anything for our patients that was needed, residents were paid almost nothing. So Dave, like the rest of us, wondered from time to time if things were better at some of the rich private sanitariums.

It came to pass that Dave was offered an attractive position at a posh hospital not far from Worcester. For reasons that will become apparent, I will not name the institution, but it had a fine public relations operation, a distinguished medical director, and counted many of the rich and famous among its clientele. Some of the classy private hospitals, like Shepherd and Enoch Pratt in Towson, Maryland, and The Chestnut Lodge in Rockville, Maryland, were choice places for training in intensive psychoanalytic psychotherapy. The institution that had recruited Dave was more biologically-oriented, but we had no reason to suspect that it was not on a par with the famous Maryland sanitariums. We were all pleased for Dave and somewhat envious. We had a little goodbye party, and Dave departed.

About three months later, Dave reappeared. He had been so miserable at the fancy sanitarium that he had finally called Dr. Rothschild, who welcomed Dave back to his old job. Of course the rest of us could not wait to hear what had happened.

"I just wish you could have been a fly on the wall!" he said to us. "Staff meetings were all about how to get the most money out of patients. I was assigned the job of doing five hours a week of intensive psychotherapy with a patient who was getting shock therapy three times a week. The patient had total amnesia for all our sessions! Then there was the patient who was given extra shock treatments that I did not think were called for, and it became clear to me that the reason for those extra treatments was to pad the patient's bill. I just could not take it. I can't tell you how happy I was when Rothschild took me back."

At Worcester, we may have been misguided or mistaken, but we were neither cynical nor opportunistic.

23

The Moon and Madness

The room Dorothy and I were awarded for my second year was on the second floor of the Administration building near the front of the hospital. It had two sets of windows, one opening towards the front of the hospital and the other opening towards the female wing. It was definitely a step up. The housing supplement had not quite covered the cost of our cardboard apartment atop the furniture store in Shrewsbury, so once we moved into the hospital we had more cash. In addition, the hospital bedroom was about twice the size of the entire Shrewsbury apartment. But it also brought with it two other changes Dorothy was not so enthusiastic about. The first was an unremitting exposure to the hospital food. The second was a more complete immersion in the hospital culture.

According to some old pictures in the halls, the hospital had been originally called the Worcester Lunatic Asylum. That was the topic of occasional discussion in the staff dining room. One of the more historically-oriented residents had gone through some of the nineteenth century papers and found records tabulating the lunar phases and the number of disturbances on the wards. The word "lunatic" comes, of course, from the old belief that the moon was a factor in madness, so my colleague was not surprised to find reports concluding that there was a correlation between full moons and upsets among the patients. The relation between the full moon and madness has not received much support from modern research. However, I understand that the police are convinced of such an association, and my own experience supports that belief.

Somehow, I had not been around the hospital late at night during a full moon while we lived in Shrewsbury. But shortly after we moved in, on a beautiful, warm summer night, we were treated to a full moon. From our open window to the open windows on the female wing, it must have been at least 75 yards, but we could hear an amazing chorus of screams, calls, and animal-like noises that grew as the moon rose.

Soon, however, there was one patient who was so loud and so arresting that she seemed to quiet the others. She imitated a steam locomotive in the most realistic and thorough way. She puffed up hills and coasted down the other side. She whistled at grade crossings and at stations. The imitation was so good that, had the train tracks not been so far from the hospital, it might have been taken for the real thing.

The next morning at breakfast she was, of course, a topic for conversation. A resident on the female service who knew the source of the train imitations explained, "That was Carlotta. She believes she has been reincarnated as a steam engine and quietly chugs around the ward most of the time. It's only during a full moon that she really goes all out."

On subsequent full moons, we learned to expect a performance from Carlotta. She never disappointed us.

24

Electronic Relics of the Pre-Penicillin Era

While even 50 years ago most of Worcester State was a relic of the past, some particular relics were also reminders of progress. For example, I mentioned the iron rings that had remained attached to the walls in the basement. They had supposedly been used to restrain patients. When I was at Worcester State, I saw restraint in the form of straight jackets used to move patients, but I never saw patients restrained in any manner on an ongoing basis. Instead, we relied on "quiet rooms" and hydrotherapy. "Quiet rooms" are still in use, but I will comment on hydrotherapy later, for it has disappeared as a method of sedation with the availability of effective tranquilizing drugs.

The most impressive relics were the diathermy machines that had been used in fever therapy for central nervous system syphilis. They too were reminders of progress. By the late 1940s, penicillin was making central nervous system syphilis a rare disease. In addition to routine serological tests for syphilis, we still dutifully examined the eyes of all new admissions for the telltale Argyle-Robertson pupils of syphilis. That was the name given to pupils when they responded sluggishly to light and were also unequal in size. I think I saw only one new case of syphilitic *dementia paralytica* during my residency.

The diathermy units sat like great prehistoric animals, waiting for some administrative decision to come down from Boston. They were impressive devices. Each had a control console attached to a cylinder about five feet long and about four feet in diameter, with a hole running through the middle that was large enough to hold a human being. At the end of each tube was a pallet that could be used to slide the patient inside the tube. In some ways, the diathermy units resembled modern magnetic resonance imaging units, although they functioned more like microwave ovens for humans.

In the 1920s, not long after the corkscrew-shaped bacteria or spirochete called *treponema pallidum* had been identified as the cause of syphilis, it had been noted that the spirochetes were put out of action by temperatures in the range found in humans with fever. Spontaneously occurring high fevers had occasionally caused remissions in central nervous system syphilis. This inspired the development of various methods to raise syphilitic patients' temperatures. Patients had been successfully treated for syphilis by infection with malaria and by injections of killed typhoid bacteria. However, diathermy was the safest and most easily controlled method of inducing hyperthermia.

It is difficult for the modern physician to remember how dreadful syphilis was before penicillin. The earlier arsenic-containing drugs had horrible side effects. For example, I once saw a woman who developed exfoliative dermatitis in response to an arsenical. She then sloughed off almost all her skin before she died. But, given the terrible consequences of late stage syphilis, the chance of exfoliative dermatitis was, in the heyday of arsenicals, still considered the lesser of two evils.

So when we complain about the present, it helps to remember our progress. For one thing, it helps keep up our spirits as we struggle to improve care for the mentally ill.

25

Hydrotherapy

As opposed to electric shock treatment, which interfered with psycho-therapy, the use of tubs and cold packs, known collectively as hydro-therapy, was well accepted as an adjunct to the psychotherapeutic management of psychoses. The hydrotherapy suites were down in the bowels of the hospital. They were twin rooms that had frosted windows. The floors were tiled and had drains about every 10 feet. One was for males and one was for females, and both hydrotherapy suites were in active use. Against one wall, a bank of showers stood behind a raised sill on the floor. The showers were used for washing disturbed patients, but they also had high-pressure jets and could deliver what were called "needle showers". These were used on patients that needed stimulation.

A private psychiatrist in Boston had reported excellent results treating depression with what he called the "Total Push" method. That involved mild sleep deprivation, almost constant vigorous physical activity during the day, and periodic stimulation with icy needle showers. It apparently worked, and now we know that both sleep deprivation and acute stress cause some depressions to remit. However, at Worcester we never had the staff to administer "Total Push."

The rest of each hydrotherapy room contained treatment tables, tubs and ice chests for cold packs. They were in regular use for hydrotherapy. Cold pack treatments could be life-saving for patients who were wildly overstimulated by their schizophrenia or their mania. Use of a hydro-therapy tub is shown in the 1948 movie *The Snake Pit*, while in her 1964 book *I Never Promised You a Rose Garden,* Joanne Greenberg,[1] under the *nom de plume* of Hannah Green, gives a patient's account of how cold packs were experienced by the person being treated.

Today, excited catatonic schizophrenia has almost gone the way of central nervous system syphilis, and hydrotherapy suites have gone the way of diathermy machines. In the 1940s, sometimes a patient frozen in catatonic immobility would suddenly become so wildly agitated as to get dangerously overheated. When a patient, either schizophrenic or manic, became wildly excited, we had no effective drugs. Barbiturate sedatives were notorious for producing the opposite, or so-called para-doxical, effect in some of these patients, so that instead of becoming sedated, the drugged patient became even more agitated. If given even more barbiturate, the patient could stop breathing. The anticholinergic drug scopolamine produced a paradoxical calming of some patients, but it blocked sweating and so was dangerous to use on an overactive person.

Physical restraint was thus often the best thing we had at our disposal. Straitjackets (euphemistically called "camisoles") were good for moving patients from one place to another, but a struggling patient could become dangerously hot. Some patients would calm down if left alone in a "quiet room." But in the hands of well-trained staff, cold packs were so effective that they were often the treatment of first choice.

The patient to be given a cold pack was placed on a padded table and wrapped in wet cotton blankets. Then other blankets, which had been kept in the ice chest, were wrapped around the patient to keep him or her cool but not cold. A person struggling wildly against restraining blankets can generate a lethal amount of heat in an amazingly short time, so the supervising hydrotherapist had to be very attentive. Pushing a hand down inside the blanket to test the body temperature, the hydrotherapist would judge just when to replace an old blanket with new cold one.

Sometimes the constant activity of a manic could also present a medical emergency. I remember a particularly likeable young man named Ted, who was admitted twice during my two years. He had been an "A" student and played tackle on his high school varsity team. When euthymic, that is to say when his mood was healthy, he was 6' 3", 220 pounds of charm.

As is so frequently and tragically the case, his second manic break was worse than his first, but, as a sophisticated second year resident, I was convinced I could be of more help to him on this second admission. About a week after his admission, I had a call from the ward at about 10:00 P.M. It seemed that Ted was really getting out of hand and demanding to see me. The night supervisor wondered if I would come down and see if I could help them calm him, so I slipped on my clothes and hurried down to the ward.

Just as I arrived at the big steel reinforced door to the next-to-last ward, I could hear Ted cursing and screaming. Then there was a great crash. I jumped back as the huge door tore off its hinges and landed in front of me. There on top of the door lay Ted who, with a big smile, said, "Hi-ya Doc!"

I suggested that he join me in a "quiet room," where I could do a little of what I believed was psychotherapy, but he was constantly moving and talking. Finally I realized I was getting nowhere, so I left him in the "quiet room" and went back to bed.

Ted did not sleep that night or the next. He ate and drank almost nothing, and was hoarse from shouting. The third day he began to run a fever and to look physically ill. For lack of anything better, I had him taken down to hydrotherapy for cold packs, and I sat with him while the packs were being administered.

The results were impressive. Of course he could not keep up his incessant movements swaddled in blankets, but his manic stream of speech began to slow down, too. After about half an hour, there were moments when I could speak to him while he listened. Then, for the next half hour we had an almost normal conversation. After that he said he was beginning to feel hungry, so we unwrapped him and had some food brought in. He ate ravenously, then complained of being sleepy. We took him back to the ward, and for the first time since his admission he slept in his bed. Within another week he was going home on leave.

Was his remission the result of our talking, or the hydrotherapy, or was it just the natural course of his bipolar affective disorder? We will never know, and thank heaven I do not have to think up a way to do a double-blind study of hydrotherapy. However, if I had to bet, I would put my money on the hydrotherapy. So I came away greatly impressed with the skills of the hydrotherapists, and with the magic of water.

26

The Psychoanalytic Citation

A residency at Worcester truly meant being a resident. Everyone lived in or near the hospital and shared the terrible hospital food for most meals. This was both a blessing and a curse. The hospital, on its huge grounds, was isolated from the rest of the city. In addition, outside of the Art Museum and Clark University, Worcester was not loaded with attractions. There was a local joke that went, "What do you think of Worcester as a hole (whole)?" Our constant association led to great camaraderie, and to an almost total immersion in the issues surrounding the treatment of the mentally ill. Residents felt they were learning at warp speed because there was nothing else to do.

With physicians, psychologists, physiologists, social workers, occupational therapists, nurses, and so on, the staff was diverse enough to provide a variety of points of view, so that the pressure cooker effect was mitigated to a degree. But the psychologists, nurses, social workers, and occupational therapists were almost as much into psychoanalytic theory as the residents, so mealtime discussions could get pretty turgid. The analytic pundits of the day were reverently quoted, and anyone making an inadvertent a slip of the tongue was quickly offered an array of free psychoanalytic interpretations.

Of course the conversations did not always have to do with analysis. There were the usual discussions of research and of various technical topics. Those tended to go on between a few people. But discussions of particular cases and of psychoanalytic theory would usually draw in everyone at a given table.

The give-and-take discussions of cases, I believe, contributed to patient care. Later I worked at a Veteran's Administration hospital where there was no dining room set aside for staff. Administrators had abolished it because they felt it gave a bad elitist message to the patients, so staff and patients all ate together. Of course, the likelihood of having a patient sitting in the next booth effectively stifled case discussions at meals. That, I think, is another example of administrators putting appearances before function.

For the few spouses who were not professionally involved in the work of the hospital, mealtimes could be a bit of a drag. From time to time there would be attempts to introduce some non-psychiatric topic, but mostly the doses of work-related information were continuous and heavy. Dorothy has always been adverse to being left out, but her background in the fine arts seemed to be keeping her on the conversational sidelines during a lot of the psychoanalytical discussions. For a while, she seemed to be weathering it like a good soldier. Finally, she had had it.

At one lunch we were being served hot dogs for the meat course. That, incidentally, was one of the better meat dishes provided by the hospital kitchen. One of the female residents was a bit on the tough side and seemed to dominate her husband, who was also a resident. The rest of us had eaten our fill, but there was one sausage left on the table, and so after looking around, the lady in question helped herself to it. At that, one of the more provocative male residents piped up with; "Do you suppose penis envy could make someone particularly fond of wieners?" The lady doctor retorted, "Could castration anxiety cause someone to make such a remark?"

At that point, my long-suffering wife spoke up. "Anna Freud has said that much too much has been made of both penis envy and castration anxiety. The modern ego psychologists say Fenichel's equating the column of feces with the penis and other such so-called deep interpretations are absurd. Anything can be put in the service of the ego, whether it's having a penis or not having a penis!"

Everyone looked at Dorothy in stunned silence, and the meal was finished with only a smattering of small talk. We went up to our room together, and before I returned to the ward I asked her, "Where in the world did you read the stuff you were talking about at the table?"

Dorothy laughed. "I just made it up," she said. "I've been listening and I don't think any of you know what you are talking about most of the time, so I decided I'd join in. How'd I do?"

I trudged off to work with some sobering thoughts going through my head. I'm not sure, but I think this is the first inkling I had that for at least some psychoanalytic theory, someone had just "made it up" out of whole cloth, as it were.

27

A Saint for the Schizophrenics

The visitors who came to the Hospital for the edification of the residents were, for those of us with professional aspirations, more than enough compensation for the lousy food. Luminaries from Boston came over for the afternoon, but those from "West of the Hudson" often stayed over for several days.

All the residents were wannabe-analysts, and for those who worked with psychotic patients, their patron saint was Frieda Fromm-Reichmann. Her sensitive essays on the psychotherapy of schizophrenics are now probably unknown to modern psychiatrists. Ever since the pioneering studies of the late Phillip Mays, the high cost/benefit ratio associated with the psychoanalytic treatment of schizophrenia has made the subject almost academic. In the book *I Never Promised You a Rose Garden*, mentioned in the last chapter, the author immortalized Frieda's gift of working with psychotic patients. It is also well known that the author was one of Frieda's patients, and under a pseudonym, figured prominently in some of Frieda's clinical essays.

Frieda lived and worked at the Chestnut Lodge in Rockville, Maryland, so she was with us for about three days. She was of course spared the hospital food, and select groups were allowed to take her out for meals each day.

She was a physically unimposing figure. Being a bit on the dumpy side, with a quiet, gentle way about her, she stood in striking contrast to her ex-husband, the prolific author Erick Fromm, who was neither dumpy nor quiet. However, her face betrayed a quick observant mind, while at the same time she radiated almost incredible warmth and acceptance. I have met other people who had charisma, and found it all too often associated with great personal narcissism. Not so with Frieda. It was as though she saw herself and the world exactly the way they were, and still loved it all.

Twice a day, she interviewed a schizophrenic patient before the residents, and then explained her theories and techniques. Some of her points were a little involved, but she would then give a reprise of such clarity that making outline notes was a snap.

We had all read most of her papers and had tried many of her techniques. In one paper, she had described sitting on the floor of a "quiet room" with a mute patient day after day until finally the patient had offered her a urine-soaked cigarette. She had given one of her clean cigarettes to the patient and together they had smoked. Then at last the patient had begun to talk.

One of the residents was in the process of trying just that and told Frieda about his attempts at imitating her. With her soft slight German accent she said, "I'm so sorry, but zat was a mistake I made long ago. Ve all make mistakes, you see. Ze problem is that sooner or later ve get tired of sitting in a 'quiet room' smoking urine soaked cigarettes. Ve must accept our limitations like ve accept those of our patients. I now think that ve should not promise a patient something that ve are not willing to deliver forever. Otherwise ve will be tested until ve fail and so fulfill their paranoid predictions."

Frieda's willingness to acknowledge an error and to explain how she had learned from the experience made a deep impression on me, for it contrasted so with the omniscient postures that some of the psychoanalytic superstars adopted. But I guess I figured that Frieda was so obviously brilliant and gifted that she could afford to learn from her mistakes. Unfortunately, I think it was only later when I realized that I could not afford NOT to learn from my mistakes.

We all fell deeply in love with Frieda and unconsciously began to develop soft German accents. Having been born and raised in Georgia, I must have sounded ludicrous, but no one seemed to notice. Then her visit came to an end. Rothschild used a lottery to settle the arguments over who would have the privilege of driving her to the train station. I won.

I was planning a move to the University of Maryland and intended to start my required personal analysis in Baltimore, so I wanted Frieda's advice about local analysts and the two competing psychoanalytic institutes. Having her to myself during the trip to the Worcester train station was a prize beyond all imagining.

We got into my car with plenty of time to spare and started towards the station. We were talking, and I was in seventh heaven when we ran into one of Worcester's famous traffic gridlocks. Soon we were immobilized in a sea of automobiles that had been trapped in one of the city's most notorious five-way intersections.

I was feeling awful thinking she might miss her train. I stopped talking and began to look around frantically although I did not know exactly what I hoped to see. Frieda quickly sized up the situation both in the traffic and in my mind. Ever so gently she said to me, "Zere iss no magic. Talk."

Suddenly, I was at ease and pleased at having this extra time with her. We were talking happily when the traffic jam broke up and we arrived at the train station with a few minutes to spare. Frieda's ability to grasp what was on the mind of a schizophrenic and to think of a supportive remark was legendary. Her ability to do the same trick with a neurotic resident was even more amazing to me.

In looking up the exact citation for *I Never Promised You a Rose Garden*, I went to Amazon.com, and there found a comment on the book by the author:

> "I wrote this book as a way of describing mental illness without the roman- ticisation that it underwent in the sixties and seventies when people were taking LSD to simulate what they thought was a liberating experience. During those days, people often confused creativity with insanity. There is no creativity in madness; madness is the opposite of creativity, although people may be creative IN SPITE of being mentally ill."

Today, antipsychotic drugs can at times relieve some of the symptoms of schizophrenia. In my experience, the new atypical antipsychotics help more without some of the side effects of the older drugs, although at the moment there is some controversy concerning the superiority of the newer dugs. The atypical antipsychotic clozaril (Clozarpine) has been shown to reduce the suicide rate in schizophrenics, but all the drugs still leave a lot to be desired, and in general,, the suicide rate of schizophrenics remains disturbingly high. There has been speculation that recovered schizophrenics clearly see their lives as having been irreparably ruined by the disease, and hence kill themselves. Certainly the lessons Frieda taught about how to help patients face and accept the experience of psychosis are still as valuable today as they were then. But some of what she said came so much from the heart that it also inspires us to listen with a different ear.

28

Deafness and Despair

With Frieda as our goddess, we all dreamed of leading schizophrenics back to health. When that proved difficult with our hospitalized patients, we hoped to find someone so early in the schizophrenic process that there would be no fixed delusional systems blocking our therapeutic efforts. I had one such opportunity.

We saw some outpatients at Memorial Hospital, the medical center in the city of Worcester. There were also some outpatients we saw at the state hospital for follow up visits after discharge. But there was one patient who was referred directly to the Worcester State for outpatient visits by her family doctor when he discovered she was showing signs of schizophrenia. I guess he hoped we had some new miracle up our sleeves. We did not, and the memory of her remains painfully clear in the way that failures tend to stick in our minds.

She seemed, at first glance, to be an almost perfect 13-year-old girl. In those days they were referred to as "Bobby Soxers," and as per the uniform of the day she wore saddle shoes with heavy white socks turned down to the ankles. A plaid skirt and a pullover sweater completed the outfit. Her complexion was clear and her features quite pretty. Her body tended to be on the heavy side, but at her age it gave her a pleasantly healthy appearance. She would have looked like a model teenager except for the rather sad expression she wore most of the time, and except for the presence of a large hearing aid behind her left ear.

She was slow in opening up to me, but little by little the details began to come out. She had started at a new high school where there were only a few classmates from her junior high school and none of her old friends. She had always been somewhat shy, and she had made no new friends. Then she began to tell me about what she heard the other girls saying behind her back. Some of it may have had a basis in reality, for she thought that they looked at her and whispered, "Weird," as she walked past. I could imagine that happening. Other thoughts were more clearly pathological. For instance, she thought the other girls were reading her mind and making her think bad thoughts about boys.

As time passed, I helplessly observed the disease slowly blotting out the hope and promise of her young life. She became more withdrawn at home and after a time refused to go to school. She also began to complain about voices in her head even when there was no one around. There seemed to be more than one voice, but all of them were female. The voices accused her of being dirty, bad, and guilty of some vague and ill-defined offense. I listened intently, empathetically, and to no avail.

I still recall a day in early spring, full of promises for melting snow and early flowers. She sat in my office, and for the last time I felt that she was trying to communicate with me. With tears glistening in her eyes, she asked me to please make the voices stop. After that she kept her appointments, but I felt she had shut me out of her life.

Not long before I left Worcester, her parents called and said she had been admitted to a psychiatric service for adolescents in Boston, and gave me permission to talk to the hospital about their daughter. The hospital never returned my call and I heard no more about her. I was disappointed that I never had a call from her new doctor, not that I know what I could have said that would have made any difference. But even now from time to time I think that if I had just had clozapine or haloperidol or, for God's sake, even chlorpromazine, I could have done something. And I still have occasional bad dreams of that child, who should have had a life waiting for her, sitting in my office and pleading with me, "Please, Dr. Callaway, make the voices go away."

Today, we have so much to offer the schizophrenics that nothing less than first rate functioning should be acceptable as an outcome. When our results are less than perfect, it is usually the health care delivery system that is at fault. But none of the present schizophrenic patients or their therapists should have to experience the frustration and despair of that inexorable downhill course. Huntington's disease still baffles us, and inevitably progresses from depression to dementia and death, but perhaps because of its terrible predictability, it is not as frustrating and distressing to the therapist as is the young schizophrenic where one keeps hoping.

29

Coarse Brain Damage

From our take of the Freudian viewpoint, all psychiatric disorders without associated demonstrable neuropathology were assumed to spring from purely psychological roots. Therefore, those psychoses that stemmed from coarse brain diseases such as tumors, traumas, and infections were referred to as "organic" psychoses. Recently, a colleague quipped, "Organic psychoses? Have you ever seen an inorganic psychosis? In fact, do 'droids' ever get psychoses?"

That anachronistic nomenclature lingers on, but 50 years ago it had more meaning, and Dr. Kurt Goldstein was the preeminent authority on organic psychological disorders. As one of the era's guiding lights, Goldstein was duly invited to spend a day with the residents at Worcester. On popular demand, many of the local psychologists also came to hear him, probably because he was co-inventor of the Goldstein-Scheerer test. That was a battery of psychological tests that, at the time, provided the most sensitive indication of coarse brain disorder. It also was of localizing value when a lesion was restricted to one part of the brain. Such lesions were called "focal."

Goldstein had written extensively on the subject, and had in particular described a syndrome in which afflicted patients showed much more psychopathology than could be explained by the anatomy of the lesion. This was most often seen when the speech areas on the dominant (usually left) side of the brain were involved. Goldstein had coined the term "catastrophic reaction" to characterize that syndrome.

I had a patient who had been found wandering and disoriented. He would occasionally and explosively utter an expletive, like "shit," but we could not get any personal information from him. That inability to utter anything but an expletive is known as jargon aphasia. He was well dressed, so we assumed someone had robbed him of his wallet, and with it, his identity. Physical examination was unremarkable, but the EEG (in one of the few examples of its utility in a mental hospital) showed focal "slow waves" coming from the left temporal area, suggesting a space-occupying lesion in the speech areas.

In spite of having no one to give consent, we risked a pneumoencepha-logram, and found radiographic evidence of the suspected left temporal lobe tumor. I was agitating for us to call in the neurosurgeon, but Rothschild urged me to try a little longer to get a name and address from the patient, and he tactfully suggested that in the long run identification might be more important than neurosurgery. So I tried some more and failed some more.

When Goldstein arrived for his visit to Worcester, he asked to have a patient that he could use to demonstrate some of his ideas. My patient with the parietal tumor and no name was the obvious choice.

What I witnessed was nothing less than a miracle. Goldstein put one hand on the patient's shoulder and another on his leg. His empathy for the man was almost palpable. With his face close to the patient's, he slowly and gently began to talk, massaging leg and shoulder in time with his words. "What is your name?"

The patient looked anguished and explosively said, "Shit!"

"That's all right. Just relax and do not try so hard. Now let's try again. What is your name?"

After several similar cycles, the patient started to get the beginnings of a word out. Then, slowly and to our astonishment, the patient began to speak. Over the next few minutes, he gave us his name and address. Goldstein had him sent back to his ward and began to explain more about the procedure.

As wannabe psychoanalysts, we scrupulously kept our hands off our patients, and did physical examinations only on patients that were assigned to someone else for psychotherapy. Timidly, we commented on what Goldstein had done. So he explained, "The patient is overwhelmed by what is happening to his mind, and you need all the help you can muster to get through the panic. I use visual, verbal, and tactile input together to reinforce each other."

I suppose it was natural for Goldstein's obvious tact and empathy to remind us of Frieda Fromm-Reichmann. While I had a natural gift for putting my foot in my mouth that the first year of residency had not modified, this time it was my dear friend and similarly gifted fellow resident, Bill Hauseman, who asked, "Dr. Goldstein, your way with patients reminds me of Dr. Fromm-Reichmann. Did you study under her?"

The great man exploded. "She vas my pupil!"

The ever-tactful Rothschild hurried the great man from the room. Later, Rothschild's clinical judgment was also confirmed. The unfortunate patient turned out to have a rapidly growing glioblastoma, and even today those are almost invariably fatal. However, at least we were able to inform his family, who took him home so he did not have to spend his last days in a state hospital.

30

Psychosomatic Medicine

One of the second-year perks was the privilege of doing outpatient psychotherapy with non-psychotic patients at the general hospital in downtown Worcester. The clinic was held one evening a week so as not to conflict with our duties at the state hospital, and there we expected to be able to apply some of the more plausible psychoanalytic theories.

50 years ago, you would have been labeled a nut or worse if you claimed an infectious microorganism caused peptic ulcers. While now I know that infection with *Helicobacter pylori* is the etiological agent in most cases of stomach ulcers, the concept of unresolved oral dependency needs still seems a much a more plausible explanation. After all, stomach ulcers respond to frequent feeding with cream, and that sounds more like a treatment of the inner child's longing for breast feeding than a treatment for a bacterial infection.

One night, my outpatient of the evening arrived with the following referral slip:

> *White, Tomas L., WMM 24, CC epigastric pain, PX neg., GI workup neg.*
> *Ref. To psych. At patient's request.*

It became immediately apparent to me that Tom White was intelligent and well-read. Thus, I thought it perfectly natural for him to suspect deep psychological problems were at the root of his otherwise unexplained epigastric distress. He was a young man of about my age who had been discharged from the Marines about three years earlier. After marrying his boyhood sweetheart, he had done two years at the Polytechnic Institute under the GI Bill and then started his own camera shop. As he explained it, he had everything he had dreamed about in the foxholes during the Pacific campaign. His college degree, his wife, and his shop were exactly as he had imagined them, so he could not understand what was going on with him to make his stomach hurt.

Since his family and past history were so unremarkable, I spent the end of our first session asking him about his work. He described his shop with pride, but explained that he was undercapitalized, as is usually the case with new businesses. Each month he tensely did the accounts and prayed he would have enough cash to service the loans he had made to start his shop. His wife stayed at home because that had been part of his dream, and he was reluctant to share his anxieties because he thought she looked on him as a hero who could do anything.

Just at the end of the session, I could not restrain myself from committing a psychoanalytic "no-no." "Tom," I said, "do you really think your wife wants to be kept in the dark about what you are feeling?"

Tom paused, and then replied, "I don't know."

"Well. See you next week," I said and let him out of the office.

The next week he came in and said, "Well, let's get started." He leaned back in his chair and began, "The earliest thing I can remember is..." Then, for the next five sessions he gave me a detailed account of his life. I was impressed by how healthy he seemed. In fact, I thought he was in better shape psychologically than I was. His family had been loving, supportive, and proud of his success in competitive sports. While not an outstanding scholar, he had done well enough in school and had been generally popular. He had started dating his wife in high school and never really considered any other woman. Right after Pearl Harbor, he had enlisted in the Marines. Boot Camp and combat in the Pacific had apparently left amazingly few scars and instead had generally reinforced his image of himself as a sort of superman.

On the seventh session, he came in, added a few missed details, and concluded, "Well, that about wraps it up."

"But what about the stomach pains?" I asked.

"Oh, they stopped after the first session. My wife asked me what we'd talked about and I told her, including your question about what she'd feel if I told her about my worries. She's so great. She said she knew I was worried but did not know how to get me to talk about it. She's working at the shop now, and I think we've turned the corner financially."

"Then why," I asked, "did you go on with psychotherapy?"

"Oh, I read that if you do not work through a conflict completely, then it will crop up in other symptoms and I did not want that to happen."

"Well, you've done a thorough job," I said.

"Thanks, Doctor," he said. We shook hands and he departed.

In retrospect, I might have been a little intrusive in the first session, but it was not far from what would be called for in modern Interpersonal Psychotherapy. The following seven sessions were fascinating to me, but I wonder if they did Tom any good. Well, they didn't cost him anything and didn't hurt him.

Primum Nul Nocere. ("First, do no harm." A traditional medical aphorism.)

31

The Magic Mirror

Today, it would be criminal for a physician to simply watch the course of schizophrenia. Fifty years ago we had no other alternative. Schizophrenia is a devastating illness, both for patient and family. Even when the disease remits, as it does occasionally, helping the patient find the least destructive way of coping with having been "crazy" is a daunting task for even the most sensitive and experienced therapist. The longer lunacy is allowed to continue, the harder it is for patients to pick up their lives if the disease does remit. On the other hand, today a schizophrenic can look forward to a productive and rewarding life if treatment is begun soon enough, if the family can be calm but firm, and if the patient can deal with the difficult issues of having a chronic illness, not the least of which is medication compliance. But for those of us treating schizophrenia, we have to be alert to novel issues that our new powerful drugs uncover.

Back in the days when we had little to offer the schizophrenic other than respect and compassion, we saw some remissions that were just as inexplicable as the illness itself. A particular case in point was Joseph, a big thirty-ish Irishman with a wild and florid delusional system. He was convinced that an atom bomb was hidden somewhere in the hospital and spent his waking hours searching for it. His delusions left him no time for personal hygiene. Because of his size, getting him showered and shaved were major enterprises for the staff, so most of the time he looked pretty disreputable.

At the time, Dr. Sidney Sands was Research Director, and he had given my wife, Dorothy, a job as secretary on the research ward. Almost every day as she sat typing, Joseph would come by to search her wastepaper basket and her desk drawers. He always explained that he was protecting her from the hidden atom bomb.

One day Joseph came by when Dorothy was away from her desk, so he gave the room a particularly thorough search. In so doing, he opened her purse and found himself staring into a mirror. Dorothy returned at that point and watched with fascination. Joseph, who was ordinarily in constant motion, was now standing still, looking at the mirror, and shaking his head in a bewildered way. When he saw Dorothy standing there, he hung his head, said, ''I'm a mess,'' and left.

We learned that, to the amazement of one and all, he had presented himself at the barbershop for a shave and haircut. Then he had returned to the ward where he requested a shower and clean clothes. Within days he was home on leave and shortly after that he was discharged. I spent some time interviewing him when he was being discharged, but he seemed as mystified by his psychotic episode as I was.

For the next few weeks I carried a mirror around with me and tried it on a random selection of psychotic patients. Needless to say, Joseph remains the only schizophrenic I know of for whom the mirror was actually magic.

32

The Dark Side

When Dorothy became secretary on the research ward, she gave me another view of the patients and the ward structure. The preceding story of Joseph and the mirror was, for both of us, one of our more pleasant recollections. Unfortunately, some shared recollections are not so pleasant.

For the most part, Worcester was an enlightened institution. It was governed by dedicated professionals, staffed by gifted nurses and attendants, and served as a training ground for enthusiastic, idealistic residents such as myself. But it had a dark side. For whenever there is a helper/helpless situation, as with guards and prisoners, sadists are attracted to it like bears to honey.

Mr. O'Connor was a night nurse on the male unit. He was a short, stout man with a balding head and scrubbed ruddy complexion. His clothes were always starched and pressed, as was his white attendant's coat. He was unmarried. He came to work early and stayed late after work. As nearly as anyone could tell, the hospital was the most important thing in his life.

The other player in this tragic duet was a tiny black cross-dressed hebephrenic patient known as Sally. The term *hebephrenia* referred to the child-like behavior of a class of schizophrenics. Sally had been picked up by the police because of bizarre behavior associated with attempts to solicit work as a female prostitute. Being dressed as a woman when he was admitted, he came first to the female service. The routine physical examination revealed a normal male body, so he was promptly transferred to the male side.

Even on the male side Sally continued to maintain that he was a woman. He talked in a high falsetto, minced about in a parody of femininity, and constantly pestered the nurses for Kotex. The delusions concerning his gender were part of an extensive, poorly organized, and rather childish paranoid system. His symptoms proved totally resistant to all the usual treatments, including insulin shock, and he was living on the research service while we puzzled about his bizarre syndrome.

Meanwhile, Sally's silly but harmless behavior made him something of a pet on the ward.

One night I was away on one of the various extramural training outings that were offered to the residents. I think it was an evening when four of us were presenting psychotherapy cases to a distinguished Boston psychoanalyst at his lovely home in Belmont, an up-scale Boston suburb. Dorothy had gone back to the research office after supper to finish some things for Dr. Sands. She was standing at a filing cabinet behind a door with the unintentional result that she was hidden from anyone passing by. As she stood there, she heard the sounds of the door from the next ward being opened, then closed and locked. Next she heard the voice of O'Connor and the terrified whimpering of Sally.

O'Connor was slapping Sally and cursing him with phrases like "filthy queer" and "piece of shit!" Sally was crying and pleading for mercy. Dorothy was horrified but remained hidden for fear of what O'Connor might do to her if he discovered she had been listening.

After a time, when he had apparently tired of abusing the little patient, O'Connor led his captive on through the office section of the research unit and on to the ward where patients were housed. Dorothy waited until she was sure the coast was clear and then hurried back to the residents' quarters. There she found Tony Vargebedian, one of the senior residents. Still shaking from her experience she unburdened herself to him.

Tony listened calmly to Dorothy, reassured her by saying she had done exactly the right thing, and promised he would look into the matter promptly. The next day nothing was said about the incident, but O'Connor was not on duty the next night. Then, a few days later, Tony told us the whole story. He had quietly asked several patients about O'Connor and found he had opened a floodgate of complaints. Sally was not the only one who O'Connor had been abusing. He had picked out patients with such bizarre delusions that anything they said was likely to be ignored even by the other patients, and he had further kept his victims quiet by threatening them with reprisals if they told anybody about what he was doing.

Tony had gone to Dr. Flowers, the superintendent, and reported both the episode with Sally and the complaints he had elicited from other patients. Dr. Flowers had suspended O'Connor, and had told Tony to assemble a panel of witnesses for a disciplinary hearing. The evening after being told about the upcoming hearing, O'Connor had gone home and hanged himself. Dorothy was naturally upset but, the staff community rallied round and reassured her that she had no cause for self-reproach.

How O'Connor's sadism could have gone undetected for so long amazed me. We thought patient/staff communication had been going along just fine. We had patient therapy groups and had conducted some of the early experiments with therapeutic communities in which staff and patients interacted quite freely. But the O'Connor affair confronted us with the fact that, while Worcester was probably better than most mental hospitals of the time, it was still far, far from ideal.

Today I watch disturbed schizophrenics wandering the streets as homeless vagrants, and I know many of them will exercise their civil liberty, demand freedom, and end up by being murdered, starved, frozen to death, or poisoned by bad street drugs. Others will be taken into the penal system where at least they will be fed, even if not protected from street drugs. There they may also refuse treatment, and often if they do get treated, they are released without adequate medical follow-up.

Can we do without some sort of asylum for the disorganized, the disruptive, and the potentially disruptive citizens who at the moment are not an "immediate danger to themselves or to others"? With medication and well-run support groups, we know that a large percentage of people who need a period of care away from the stress of the public world can be returned to gainful participation in the community's life. But just as it is curious how O'Connor got away with his behavior, it is equally curious why we do not use what we already know about treating mental patients. So, how many more Sallys will meet up with how many more O'Connors in the mean streets?

33

Behind the Wall of Silence

I cannot remember the last time I saw a truly catatonic patient. I asked a colleague from New York about that. He is heavily involved in the management of psychotic patients, and he also had a hard time remembering the last one he saw. On the other hand, I belong to an e-mail "list-serve" that deals with issues in psychopharmacology, and there I have found that colleagues from foreign countries and even some of our poorer states still see catatonics being admitted to mental hospitals.

I had wondered if the antipsychotic medications and the benzodiazepine tranquilizers made catatonics a thing of the past, or whether, with the passing of warehouse-like asylums, there is nowhere for the schizophrenic to fully develop that strange syndrome. Those seem unlikely explanations. I know for certain that the energetic nurses we had at the Langley Porter Institute (University of California San Francisco) in the 1960s and 1970s would simply not allow a patient to get away with catatonic behavior in their presence, but that still does not explain the absence of catatonia in new admissions.

Recently, some colleagues suggested that catatonia has been swallowed up in other diagnoses. One of those colleagues suggested that most of the cases described in the old literature would now be diagnosed as bipolar affective disorders (manic-depressives) or organic brain syndrome. Another felt that most now would be diagnosed as having neuroleptic malignant syndrome. That is a condition where muscles throughout the body, including those around hair follicles, contract. This often leads to muscle damage and can raise the body temperature so high as to be lethal in some cases.

It is most dramatic as a side-effect of treatments with the older antipsychotic drugs and older anesthetic agents, but can make its appearance without any apparent cause. There is quite a literature about muscle abnormalities in schizophrenia that cause elevated temperatures. On the other hand, when I was at Worcester, there was no shortage of catatonics who had always had normal temperatures. As is usually the case when there are a lot of explanations, none of them are entirely satisfactory.

In any case, half a century ago catatonics were plentiful. There were some in the main hospital. They were younger and more acute, so we could still hope that some of them might recover. But the real collection was housed at the old original hospital, then known as the Summer Street division. They had one ward almost full of those immobile, silent sufferers. Although they did not speak, there were some whose fingers were blue from peripheral vasoconstriction and whose pupils were widely dilated. Those autonomic signs suggested some awful inner terror. Others looked as if they were seeing some vision of ultimate bliss. Some showed the so-called waxy flexibility described in the old textbooks. Their limbs could be placed in awkward postures and would stay there until, like softening wax, they slowly returned to their preferred posture. Some would sit in chairs but others would stand until their legs were swollen and discolored. Some would occasionally and for no apparent reason explode into a wild and agitated state we called "catatonic excitement."

There seemed to be no particular prognostic significance to catatonia. Some responded to insulin or electric shock treatments, and others simply stopped being catatonic for reasons that no one could fathom. The most accurate predictors of outcome were level of pre-psychotic functioning and length of illness. As in many diseases, the longer a patient is sick, the less chance there is for recovery. So the catatonics who failed to improve slowly filtered back to the Summer Street Division. All patients there were supposed to be examined by a doctor once a year, so the residents made infrequent periodic visits to Summer Street. There, chronic delusional patients sat muttering to themselves, catatonics lined the walls, and a few lost obsessive souls kept the floors gleaming by eternally running the buffing machine over them.

Early one Sunday morning when I was on call, I got an unusual request. A driver was coming over from the Summer Street Division to get me for a medical emergency. By the time I got my clothes on and got down to the porte-cochère, the driver was waiting and whisked me into Worcester and on to Summer Street where the old hospital building stood. I was hurried into a room on the first floor where I found a large young man in an attendant's uniform sitting on the floor holding his wrist. It had been a few years since orthopedic surgery in medical school, but I had no trouble diagnosing a Collie's fracture of the wrist from a distance. However, I performed a "laying on of hands" as a physician should, then told the driver to take him over to Memorial Hospital immediately while I called ahead. Then I asked the driver to return so he could take me back to the main hospital after I had finished my report.

It turned out that it was the unfortunate young man's first day on the job. No one had warned him that the waxy statues along the walls were potentially violent psychotics. He had come through the door carrying a food tray, for at the old Summer Street Division they still brought food onto the wards. The newer (1838) main hospital was one of the first mental institutions in the world to serve patients in a cafeteria. At any rate, as the young man had come on to the ward he had carelessly backed into a catatonic patient. The patient had galvanized into action, flung the young man to the floor, thus fracturing his wrist, and then returned to his former immobility.

While I was writing my accident report, I asked the head attendant if they did not give some sort of training to the people they hired. He walked away without answering me.

34

Gather Ye Labwear Where Ye May

Research going on at the state hospital and at the foundation was extensive and varied. Most of the research from those days has been published and can be found in *Index Medicus.* While many of those papers made significant contributions at the time, they are likely to be ignored today. First, research that old comes under the heading of ancient history. Second, everyone searches the literature with Medline (computer access to the National Library of Medicine), which does not index papers written before 1966. More to the point of these memoirs is the way research contributed to our sense of camaraderie, and provided a balance to the clinical work.

While I was at Worcester, at least three quarters of the residents published papers in edited journals. Since then, I have not encountered such a productive group of residents, and so I have often wondered what possessed us as a group to put in the extra time and effort required to do research and write it up. But, like most human behavior, it was probably "multiply determined." To begin with, we had the examples of the psychologists as well as physiologists and biochemists from the foundation. The psychologists were imaginative and always doing ingenious studies. Of course, they had their eyes on academic appointments and needed publications to get faculty offers. The foundation scientists were career researchers and naturally into publishing.

The infrastructure also supported research. The excellent library on the main floor of the administration building had great places to read quietly. The librarian, Dr. Banays, was knowledgeable and ever helpful. There was a trap door in the middle of the library, and when we needed some obscure reference, Banays would pop down into his hidden stacks and emerge with the needed document.

There was an enormous patient population and remarkably good clinical records, courtesy of the Schizophrenia Research Project, which had been based at Worcester from 1924 to 1944. So, for instance, if someone noticed a psychotic patient improving during an asthma attack, it was possible to go back and gather a reasonable sample of psychotic patients with asthma to see if recovery from psychosis during an acute attack was a common phenomenon.

Finally, we enjoyed a blessed absence of interference. We lived and breathed psychiatry, so there were no distractions. When almost all of one's colleagues were passing out reprints, it was a matter of competitive spirit to get into the game. This illustrates the relative effectiveness of peer pressure as opposed to top-down attempts at motivation. There was no active encouragement from Rothschild or Flowers to do and publish research. Indeed, carrying out a research project was usually taken as evidence that one was not being overworked and so resulted in one being assigned an additional clinical chore.

There were no grant proposals, because no one was giving grants. With no money to spend, there were no business administrators to cope with. There were no human subject committees, so when one had an idea for a study, one simply did it.

Not that we did not have people to discuss our ideas with. I became interested in the effects of methamphetamine on schizophrenics, and I discussed my ideas at length with Dr. Justin Hope, a Boston psychiatrist who was an attending physician on the research service. But when we finally decided what I should do, I simply got the drug from the pharmacy, I.V. sets from central supply, and went on the wards asking my patient-friends if they would mind me giving them a shot so I could see how it would affect them.

Of course that laissez-faire approach to research resulted in some terrible abuses later on, and now the federal Office for the Protection of Human Subjects is big business. However, they seem much more concerned with i-dotting, t-crossing, and bureaucratic empire building than with the actual protection of human subjects. In those days before word processors, when everything had to be typed by hand, the requirements of the modern bureaucracy would have shut down the works entirely.

Post WW II, and before Sputnik lit a fire under the federal government, biological research was funded largely by industry and wealthy citizens. The Office of Naval Research was an exception, but even they were not given to great outlays of cash. So the experimental psychologists built a lot of their own equipment. A bunch of "ham" radio operators ran a store in Boston called the Radio Shack and dealt largely in military surplus. I think that was the origin of the current Radio Shack empire, but I am not sure. Equipment that had cost the government thousands could be bought for a few dollars, so with a little imagination we did pretty well on the electronic front.

The gentleman in charge of equipment for the psychology lab at the hospital was a wizard at cobbling together instruments and, when there was no good military surplus source, he had an amazing cache of odds and ends that could be pressed into service. He presided over a storeroom in the bowels of the hospital and was unfailingly helpful. I had no idea that he was a patient and assumed that he was on the psychology department pay roll. One day I asked him how a man as brilliant as he was came to work at a state hospital. That question unleashed a barrage of paranoid material that I never dreamed lay beneath his ever-helpful working persona. He believed that he had invented the Beldin transmission and that the big auto companies had stolen it from him. I do not know whether or not the automobile industry had defrauded him, but the looseness of his associations gave ample evidence for the accuracy of his diagnosis as a paranoid schizophrenic.

The chemistry labs at the Foundation and the hospital were another matter. They had a glass blower, but he did only wonderfully special things. Routine items like test tubes, flasks, and distillation columns were always in short supply. One day at lunch, some of the psychologists were rejoicing over a particularly fortunate foray to the Radio Shack. One of the foundation chemists began bewailing their limited supplies of laboratory glass wear and the absence of a convenient war surplus store for their needs. Then one of the psychologists who had been an officer in the Medical Service Corps said he knew of a warehouse stuffed with laboratory glassware. He volunteered to get a truck and fill it with whatever was needed if the chemists would make a wish list and lend him a clipboard.

The list was duly prepared and the young ex-officer disappeared with list and clipboard. The next afternoon a big army truck pulled up in front of the foundation. The psychologist, now in 1st lieutenant's uniform, got out, along with three enlisted men. After directing them to unload the truck-full of laboratory equipment, he officiously asked one of the chemists to sign the sheet on the clipboard. Then he and his enlisted men got back in the truck and departed.

A few hours later he reappeared in civilian clothes. The clipboard was the secret, he explained. First he had gone to the motor pool and commandeered the truck, having the sergeant sign a sheet on the clipboard when he took the vehicle. Then he went by a holding company and picked up the three enlisted men. Next, he went to the warehouse, and with clipboard in hand he directed the enlisted men to load the selected items into the van. Then he had the sergeant in charge of the warehouse sign the clipboard again. Having unloaded the loot at the foundation, he returned the men to their holding company, returned the van to the motor pool, and had the sergeant sign the clipboard yet again. He proudly displayed the clipboard with a sheet that had been duly signed by all the sergeants involved. Then he relaxed to bask in the gratitude and admiration of the chemists.

A colleague reading an earlier version of this memoir asked if I meant to imply that today's researchers lack the necessary psychopathy to come up with devious solutions. Of course they do not. But I do wonder if they enjoy the same sense of playful improvisation that we did.

35

Miscellaneous Misadventures

This spirit of improvisation did not always end in such success, and I can recall incidents to illustrate the flip side of the freedom we enjoyed. In two of them, I was on my own. These two stories are concerned with my excursions into do-it-yourself audio engineering. The other two involved most of the other residents.

My experience in repairing the EEG machine released the repressed engineer in me, and with help and encouragement from one of the foundation polymaths, I set out to build myself a high fidelity sound system from surplus parts. On one occasion, I had slipped back to my room in the middle of the day to finish soldering the amplifier chassis. In the next room, a conference of hospital administrators was in progress. I was so engrossed in my soldering that I inadvertently picked up the soldering iron by the hot end. With the big brass in the next room, I could not cry out, so, biting my tongue, I scurried over to the infirmary for first aid.

Then, when I started testing my system with the help of a borrowed signal generator, I was distressed to find that inputs above about 11,000 hertz produced no output that I could hear, even with the volume turned up to the maximum. I was wondering where I had gone wrong when a neighbor burst into my room shouting, "Turn that dam thing off before we all go nuts!" Subsequent audiological tests revealed that I had a severe high frequency hearing loss, presumably the result of my fascination with firearms as a youngster.

Then there was the time we decided to boost the alcohol content of our applejack. Apple cider left indoors became slightly carbonated and mildly alcoholic. The alcohol concentration could be enhanced somewhat by putting it outside on the windowsill. Freezing the fermented cider allowed us to pour the high alcohol liquid off the top of the frozen part. But with chemistry labs right at hand, we thought we could continue to improve our product by distilling it. We ran off a sample with cold water running through the distillation column, but to our horror the result was a foul either-like liquid. Reading after the fact, I learned that operating a liquor still is an art. The temperature of the column must be just right so that the highly volatile either-like components are boiled off and the desired alcohols and congeners come through. I also learned that corn "licker" connoisseurs (and some revenue officers) can tell by the taste of the "white lightning" which bootlegger made that particular batch of moonshine.

There was another improvisational adventure that ended more satisfactorily. The quality of our food was such that, in the winter, our craving for red meat became almost pathological. So we talked the dietician into helping us buy a standing rib roast and lending us the use of one of his huge ovens on a Sunday, when the hospital kitchen was closed,. Great communal preparations were underway in anticipation of the rare beef when the dietician returned to see if we needed any help. The roast was just coming out, but the dietician was horrified. He said beef so rare would make us all sick and tried to make us put it back in the oven until it was dark brown all the way through. Dr. Rothschild, the clinical director, and Dr. Flower, the superintendent, were away at the time. It was only through the intervention of Dr. Sands, the director of research, that our precious roast was saved from becoming grey and tasteless, like the meat we were accustomed to.

36

The Fortunate Failure

A study is called "double-blind" when neither the experimenter nor the subject knows which is the active treatment and which is the placebo or control treatment. This type of study is so much a part of the pharmaco-therapeutic culture that an "open label" drug trial (everybody knows who is getting the drug) is considered nothing more than a pilot study. This next story concerns a time when double-blind studies were not taken for granted, and an experience that left me a true believer in the double-blind.

Lest some modern sophisticated reader think that, today, "double-blind" is such an obvious requirement that the next story is only of historical interest, I want first to tell about a recent personal experience. A distinguished scholar from the physical sciences had reason to suspect that a particular electromagnetic field had immediate effects on the human central nervous system. He asked my help in designing a study, but when I insisted on some sort of double-blind control, he argued, "My subjects will be too intelligent to have placebo responses."

He had rigged up a rudimentary skin resistance meter and a field generator. He was showing me how, when he turned on the field, his skin resistance fell. I unplugged the power supply to his field generator when he was not looking and then I asked him to show me again how the field caused his skin resistance to fall. As before, when he turned on the switch of his field generator, his skin resistance fell. Then I pointed to the disconnected power supply plug which I had laid on the floor. Thus, no field had been produced when he closed the switch, yet his skin resistance had dropped just as it had before. I got no more arguments against double-blind studies from him.

Now, back to my experience of some 50 years ago. As a pre-eminent center for endocrine research, the foundation was interested in adrenal steroids as well as in sex steroids. What with the schizophrenia project, it was inevitable that they began to wonder if adrenal steroids played a role in schizophrenia.

The adrenal gland is really two glands in one. The central core or medulla produces adrenaline, the stuff that speeds your heart, stops your guts from operating, and generally gets you ready for "fight or flight." The surface part of the gland or cortex excretes steroids that play more complex roles in metabolic responses to stress. The adrenal cortex is controlled by a protein called Adreno-Cortico-Trophic Hormone, or ACTH, which is released from the pituitary gland. ACTH in turn is controlled by another protein called Corticotrophin Releasing Factor or Hormone, and abbreviated CRF or CRH. That hormone comes from a core structure in the brain known as the hypothalamus. A circuit from hypothalamus to pituitary to adrenal cortex is known as the HPA axis, and plays a crucial role in regulating the organism's response to stress.

Normally, over the course of every 24 hours or so, the secretion of adrenal corticosteroids into the blood stream changes cyclically, with a low point at about 2:00 A.M. and a high point shortly after arising in the morning. Around 1949, our methods were too insensitive to analyze steroids in small samples of blood. However, a 24-hour urine sample averaged out the diurnal cycle and gave us plenty of material for our assay.

Since corticosteroids play such a central role in the responses to stress, it seemed plausible to suspect they had something to do with schizophrenia. Now, even when steroid production is averaged over a whole day, the 24-hour output varies from person to person. On almost any measure you choose, schizophrenics show more inter-individual variations than do normal subjects. So when we wanted to find if there was anything abnormal in the adrenal function of schizophrenics, the obvious first step was to analyze a fair number of 24-hour urine specimens from schizophrenics and normals.

Getting a 24-hour urine specimen from a cooperative normal is not the easiest thing in the world. Forget to pee in the collection bag just once and you have to start over. Just imagine the problems involved in making such collections from disturbed psychotic patients. How I managed to avoid that particular a job I do not remember, but I think Fred Elmadjian was put in charge of that project.

To carry out the field operation, he recruited an indefatigably good-humored gentleman whose name escapes me now. For the purposes of this narrative, my associations suggest that I refer to him as Peter. The patients to be studied were the most disturbed and chronic schizophrenics that we could find. Since we were looking for something abnormal about adrenal function, we wanted the most abnormal subjects possible. The old term for schizophrenia was dementia praecox, or early dementia. That term suggested an inexorable progression to a deteriorated demented state like that seen in the end stages of dementia paralytica (central nervous system syphilis) and Alzheimer-type senile dementia. The patients we selected met the old definition of dementia praecox.

Such patients were notoriously cavalier about where they relieved themselves. They were dressed in canvas slacks and jackets that could be removed and washed frequently, and were housed on a ward with tile floors and drains so that everything could be hosed down and disinfected daily. In spite of the staff's best efforts, the smell of the back wards is one of my enduring memories.

Peter was assigned one patient at a time, and for 24 hours he lived by his subject's side. Of course, in those days, and for decades thereafter, research was done exclusively on males. They do not have menstrual cycles and can pee into bottles more easily. Finally, psychotic males are generally more tractable than psychotic females. Nowadays, one of the fallouts of feminism is the requirement by federal granting agencies that research projects use equal numbers of men and women. Given the disposition and anatomy that one encounters in severely psychotic females, I wonder if such a study could be done today.

The patients' dining room was in the basement and was itself not unpleasant. It had windows on three sides, but it was approached through long windowless corridors. The disturbed patients who could still feed themselves were herded down the stairs and lined up along the walls of those corridors to wait their turns at the steam tables in the cafeteria. Peter worked at urine collecting about twice a week, and for some months he was a familiar sight as he shadowed his quarry. Tall, blond, carrying his liter urine bottle, and dressed in white scrubs (colored operating room gowns were still decades away), he stood out from the crowd of sick patients.

The event I will describe occurred towards the end of the project, when even Peter's fabulous good humor was beginning to wear thin. One evening I passed him in the corridor, and, seeing him without his usual smile, I asked him, in an attempt to be solicitous, how things were going. He was turning away from his ward to answer me when we heard the sound of water falling on the tile floor. We both looked in horror to see his subject with a devilish grin on his face, peeing in his pants.

Peter's specimen jug was almost full, and it was apparently just at the end of that subject's collection period, but the volume of fluid running down the tile floor clearly made the collection incomplete. I looked back at Peter and saw tears in his eyes. There is a joke about hating to see a strong man cry. That time it was no joke.

Analyses of the laboriously collected urine showed that our schizo-phrenics had low urine corticosteroids. Later we discovered that the low cortical steroid outputs in our patients were secondary to sub-clinical scurvy, for we had done the first study in the winter when patients in the state hospital got precious little vitamin C in their diets. Meanwhile, before discovering the low vitamin C levels, we thought we had evidence that adrenal function was abnormal in schizophrenia.

We knew it did not help schizophrenics to give them adrenal steroids, and in fact those hormones could produce schizophrenic-like symptoms in normals. However, we wondered if the problem in schizophrenia might be at the level of ACTH production. We did not have the ability to measure a patient's ACTH level, but Armour Inc., the meat packing company, had isolated ACTH from animal pituitary glands and said they would supply some to see if it helped schizophrenics. They told us the drug for treating two subjects would cost them about $100,000, so they wanted a well-designed study.

I was assigned to find four matched schizophrenic patients. That way we could do a double-blind study where two would get drug and two would get placebo. At first I protested, since I knew no chronic schizophrenic would respond to a placebo, but I gave in to my betters. I thought finding four matched patients would be a snap, with 3,000 patients to choose from. In the process, I learned something about combinatorial calculations the hard way. Three weeks of steady work finally produced four male paranoid schizophrenics, with ages between 20 and 23 years, weights between 160 and 170 pounds, heights between 5'8" and 5'10", on their first hospitalization, and in hospital from one to two years. Interestingly, the four men also looked alike.

I admitted them to the research ward and did careful clinical examinations. Then, Dr. Sands, the Research Director, and I did ratings on the Malamud-Sands rating scale each day to try to quantify the degree of illness. Every day Dr. Harry Freeman, the foundation's attending endocrinologist, came in and gave each of the four patients an intramuscular injection of something in peanut oil. Two were presumably placebos, and two contained active hormone. He avoided talking to anyone lest he influence the outcome. He just came, gave his shots, and left.

The research staff held their breaths. Then two patients began to improve. They stopped talking about their delusions, became attentive to their personal hygiene, and began doing occupational therapy projects. The other two, if anything, got worse.

Soon, excitement on the ward was palpable, and with it the improving patients got even better. Almost every day, either Hoagland or Pincus would arrive with some dignitary in tow, chat with the four subjects, and depart. I certainly was convinced that ACTH was curing schizophrenia, and that breaking the blind would be an anticlimax. We were all bracing for reporters, movie cameras, and instant fame.

Then one day the head nurse called my attention to something when I was doing my daily exams. Two subjects were developing acne and curious fat deposits. Their faces were taking on a moon-like appearance and they were developing slight humps on their backs. "Doesn't that look like Cushing's disease?" she asked.

Cushing's disease is caused when the adrenal cortex puts out excessive amounts of steroids. Apparently, the ACTH was stimulating the patients' adrenals to produce increased amounts of steroids. This was resulting in the signs of Cushing's disease, just as one might expect if the dose of ACTH was high enough. But only one of the "improved" patients had the signs of Cushing's disease. One of the unimproved and supposed "placebo" patients also had those signs.

There was only one explanation for why the patient without a sign of ACTH effects had shown such a dramatic improvement. The enthusiastic response of the ward to the patients that we thought were getting the active drug had produced a powerful placebo effect. Although it was two more days before Freeman would break the blind, we all knew the experiment had been a failure. The gloom and disappointment on the ward became as pervasive as had been the excitement. Then the reverse placebo effect became evident as both of the two "improved" patients succumbed to the contagious depression afflicting the research ward, and regressed back to their pre-treatment states. Meanwhile, I had the unhappy job of talking to the families of schizophrenics who had heard rumors about our "cure" for that awful disease.

After the blind was broken and we had written our report, I was sitting at my desk looking quite disconsolate. Harry Freeman came in and sat down across from me.

"Don't look so glum, Noch. Just think how bad it could have been."

"What do you mean?" I asked.

"Well," he replied, "The two responders could have, by chance, both been on ACTH. Then we'd have spent millions on a big study, and gotten a lot of poor people excited about a promise we couldn't keep. Always remember, in research, there is nothing wrong with being wrong."

37

He Who Calls His Neighbor a Fool

Our intimate group of residents, psychologists, and other health-related professionals had great fun together, but we also had a tragedy that still bothers me. I have been told that, according to the Bible, "He who calls his neighbor a fool is in danger of hell fire and damnation." I was also told that is why the Quakers say "Fourth Month Dunce Day" instead of April Fools Day. Be that as it may, I think that all of us have a general inclination to assume that people are reasonable, and to deny that they are "foolish." But mental health professionals in particular are often surprisingly insensitive when it comes to detecting serious psychological problems in their colleagues.

Over the years, several of my colleagues have committed suicide when neither my other fellow psychiatrists nor I suspected that they were depressed. But then, experienced psychotherapists are good at hiding feelings. We had no such excuse for ignoring Ruthie's problem. She was just beginning her psychology training, and was as open as flowers in spring. And I hope she did not end in a suicide.

The psychology department at Worcester State was outstanding. Doctoral candidates from several universities came there for training, and members of the Worcester State staff regularly departed from Worcester for prestigious university faculty positions elsewhere. The residents were generally in awe of the Ph.D. psychologists, who obviously knew so much more about things psychological. For example, once a year, Les Phillips gave an evening class at Clark University on the Rorschach test, and as a special treat, some of us residents were allowed to go in and audit the class.

Ruthie was a psychology graduate student who was doing some of her training at Worcester State. She was a pretty young woman with a sweet personality and naturally curly blond hair that was lovely even though she seemed to pay it absolutely no attention. The other women envied her for her hair, but other than that everybody loved her.

As a courtly southern gentleman, the line between my being courteous and being flirtatious was sometimes unclear. Ruthie was certainly an attractive young woman, but there was something fragile about her that completely inhibited my flirtatious tendencies where she was concerned.

She had been assigned to a therapy group I had for schizophrenic patients, so I got to know her a bit. The patients were relatively intact, and it was summertime, so on warm, sunny days we often had our group sessions on the lawn in front of the hospital. Great old trees were scattered about the well-kept lawns, and there were many inviting places where groups could settle themselves for discussions. The patients in my group, of course, made strange remarks from time to time, reflecting their fluctuating hallucinations and delusions, but the group sessions were generally pretty mellow. We, of course, tried to "resonate" with the patients' delusional systems, as was the style at the time. That is to say, we would try to empathize with a patient's delusion and then probe into what we thought might be its psychogenesis. It was years later, in 1969, when Nick Kanas[2] demonstrated that such intrusive group therapy for schizophrenia is counterproductive

After having been with my group for a few weeks, Ruthie began to make remarks from time to time that were even odder than my attempts to shed psychoanalytic insights on the patients' delusions. She would say things like, "The sun sees into my soul, but the moon cannot." I just thought she was interacting even more empathetically with the patients than I was.

Ruthie was also in a watercolor class that Dorothy taught for the staff on weekends, so Dorothy knew her in another context. One day Dorothy and I were talking with another resident and his wife when Dorothy said, "I think Ruthie is getting sick. She has been saying some really strange things in the watercolor class."

"Like what?" I asked.

"Like, 'Do you think there are things going on behind the paper while you are painting on it?' and 'Why do you think people want to read your mind?'"

My colleague chimed in, "I just think Ruthie has been working with schizophrenics a lot and reading too much about the psychodynamics of schizophrenic thought."

Dorothy said again, "Well, she sounds sick to me." Then she dropped the subject.

A few days later, Ruthie was missing at supper. No one had any idea where she could have gone, and after a bit of asking around, Dr. Rothschild called the police. The next morning we heard that Ruthie had been found walking well out into the Atlantic surf on the shore north of Boston. They had taken her to a hospital in Boston, wet and covered with sand, where she insisted that Felix Deutsche was psychoanalyzing her by mental telepathy. She claimed that her walk into the ocean was part of her therapy.

I have no idea what ever happened to Ruthie. Many schizophrenics are successful in killing themselves, and I hope Ruthie was not one of those. As many as 20 percent of patients with acute schizophrenia may recover and go on without further episodes, but those odds are not good.

In those days, responding to the early signs of Ruthie's illness would not have made much difference. Today, early treatment of a prodromal psychosis is critical. I wonder if early signs of mental illness among colleagues still get overlooked. Many of us have thoughts and even actions that we do not want scrutinized. Do mental health workers adopt an unconscious consensus, "I'll overlook your occasional weirdness if you will extend me the same courtesy"?

I wonder.

38

The Genital Sentinel

The big fence around the front of the state hospital grounds and the huge, fortress-like hospital did not exactly give the place a homey atmosphere. Upon taking a closer look at the hospital itself, a visitor would see bars on the windows, which further reinforced the general prison ambience. But the gate was never shut, the park between the gate and the hospital was really quite inviting, and many of the patients came and went from the hospital more or less at will.

While the staff had a private dining room, the hospital kitchens were closed on Sundays, so for lunch and dinner we were served cold food with the patients in the cafeteria on the ground floor. That consisted of bread and third rate cold cuts, accompanied by the odor of scouring powder and old dishwater. Because of that, staff and open ward patients also met on Sundays at a small roadside cafe across the highway from the front gate. There they bought snacks to supplement or replace the unappetizing hospital offerings. The *specialité de la maison* was a pork chop sandwich. Their other notable delicacy was called "The Gooey." It was constructed by taking a chocolate brownie topped with vanilla ice cream and covering the whole thing with whipped cream. Looking back, ignorance of the evil in fat was bliss.

Late one Sunday afternoon, on behalf of some of my colleagues and our spouses, I took my car and made the mile trip from hospital to café for some pork chop sandwiches. I was in a hurry and was not paying much attention to the scenery as I drove through the gate and across the road to the cafe. When I went in to pick up my order, the owner said, "Doc, did you look at the top of the gate as you came through?"

"No," I said. "Why?"

"Take a look."

I looked across the road, and there atop the stone gatepost was a small man with a large smile on his face. His pants were down around his ankles, and with his hands on his hips he was flipping his penis at the passing cars. Fortunately, the gateposts were about eight feet high so that most of the people driving by did not notice him, for otherwise he might have posed a hazard to navigation.

The café owner continued, "He's been there for about 30 minutes, so when you go back, maybe you should tell somebody."

"Of course," I said. "But how do you suppose he got up on top of that post?"

"I don't know. But he does it once or twice a year."

If one can ignore the tragic consequences that delusional systems can have on the patient's life, the delusions can be amusing and in a few cases even seem to amuse the patient. However, patients like our Gatekeeper are no longer in the mental health system. The so-called positive symptoms, such as hallucinations and delusions, are responsive to older

Scene in a Madhouse from *A Rake's Progress*, **1735 engraving by William Hogarth (1697–1764). This somewhat fanciful depiction of the Royal Bethlehem Hospital for the insane around 1700 (also known as Bedlam) was said to be surprisingly accurate by observers of the time. By the nineteenth century, and at the height of moral therapy, it had become quite a tidy place with flowers on the walls. Copyright © Museum of London**

medications such as haloperidol and phenothiazines. With the advent of those antipsychotics, the colorful if tragic madmen all but vanished from the hospitals and clinics.

The famous Hogarth etching of the Rake in Bedlam shows quite a collection of psychotic patients acting out their delusions. The picture also shows a few of the more withdrawn and less dramatic people, who were referred to as simple schizophrenics. Such negative symptoms as apathy and mutism proved resistant to the earlier drugs, so for many years a lot of patients sat around their day treatment centers in what some people referred to as "chemical straitjackets." Now, the newer atypical antipsychotics promise to bring relief from the negative symptoms, too.

Today, if you want to see people like Hogarth's madmen and our Gatekeeper, you need only look among the homeless street people.

39

Did She Die from Counter-Transference?

I have praised the benefits of both our intensive patient contacts and the pressure cooker effect of living and working with colleagues. I have also wondered if the present-day resident does not spend too much time being taught at the cost of time with patients and the literature. Of course, in my later psychoanalytically-oriented training, I got plenty of case supervision, but not at Worcester. I suspect Rothschild thought the time we spent in psychotherapy of psychotic patients was something he had to allow to keep the residents happy. In the second year we had a couple of hours every other week to discuss cases with a Boston psychoanalyst, and there were some great visiting teachers, but otherwise we discussed our cases with each other. The blind leading the blind.

So we all knew a lot about Diana. She had been presented to staff several times during her inpatient stay, she was discussed with our Boston analyst, and most of all she was agonized over by her therapist when we sat around after supper smoking cigarettes and worrying about our patients. Even on admission when she was in a suicidal depression, withdrawn and disheveled, it was obvious that she was an uncommonly beautiful young woman. I will use the name Fritz to refer to the resident assigned to her case, as there was no one among my group of residents with that name.

While she was being worked up for electroconvulsive therapy (ECT), Fritz began his idea of intensive psychotherapy, and before the ECT could be started it was clear she was improving. It was like watching a flower unfold. She had a smile that could light up a room. She was considerate of the nurses and other patients. She had a quiet, subtle sense of humor, but beneath that one could sense an underlying pain that was an effective stimulus for rescue fantasies. In short, she endeared herself to all and sundry. I had an ambivalent envy for Fritz. In some ways she was the sort of patient one dreamed of, but I doubted if I was prepared for the transference and counter transference issues that were likely to arise.

The psychoanalysts made much of the feelings, both positive and negative, that patients had for their therapists. Such feelings were generally considered to be irrational and to represent transference of infantile feelings. The therapist was to be detached, and warm feelings for the analysand were thought to be another form of transference, which was known as counter transference. One of the goals of psychoanalysis was to resolve or cure the transference neurosis in the patient, and a goal of training analysis was to immunize against counter transference.

Today we recognize that the positive feelings that arise between two people working successfully together on a difficult problem are valuable, and that analysis of the transference neurosis is not positively correlated with benefits from analysis. Second, when you put two attractive, normal, young adults of the opposite sex together who are experiencing work-related positive feelings, sexual attraction is almost inevitable.

Today the therapist is not expected to be immune, but to recognize such positive feelings and make sure they do not interfere with therapy. That stricture is not just for the benefit of the patient. I have known several analysts who divorced their wives to marry a patient. While my sample is small, the disastrous results from those second marriages suggest that the stricture against physical involvement with patients is justified both morally and from the observations of outcomes.

Although at the time I was not familiar with all the information in the above paragraphs, I nevertheless knew I was in no way ready to cope with Diana as a patient. And as I had predicted, not long before her discharge, she let it be known that she thought Fritz was the new Messiah and worshiped him accordingly. Because of the problems Diana's intense attachment to Fritz posed for her therapy, given the theories of the time, by common consent we turned our time with the Boston analyst into a continuous case seminar on Fritz and Diana.

In supervision with the Boston analyst, Fritz confessed he found himself reciprocating the feelings of this beautiful and talented young woman who said she loved him, but he hoped that by talking about his feelings he could avoid letting them influence the course of therapy. He also followed the analyst's suggestions as carefully as possible. To Diana's confessions of love, Fritz suggested she talk more about that. It then came out that she had been an unusually beautiful child, and had suffered inappropriate sexual advances from relatives and friends of the family. She asked Fritz if he loved her, and when he asked her to talk more about that, she sighed and said that she knew he loved her, but being honor-bound by his profession, the therapeutic relationship was the only one they could ever share. She told Fritz he was the only man she had ever felt safe with, so was it any wonder that she loved him so?

Diana continued to improve and soon went home on leave from the hospital. When she became an outpatient, she began bringing gifts.

She was a talented pastry cook, and considering our hospital cuisine, it was cruel and unusual punishment that Fritz inflicted on himself when, under instruction from our supervisor, he turned down her offerings. After his refusals, however, she brought the cakes and pies to the ward for the staff and patients to enjoy. We were all grateful for that.

After some months of twice-a-week outpatient psychotherapy, things began to change. Diana complained of mornings when she woke up wishing she were dead. There would be good days, but more and more it was like the early stages of her previous depressions. She began to lose weight and to be careless about her appearance. Fritz argued with himself about whether she should be hospitalized and given ECT. He was preparing to discuss that with the analyst on our next session.

Then, one morning, Gurrey at the switchboard called Fritz and told him Diana had left him an enormous Boston cream pie. Fritz was immediately alarmed and called her home. Her mother said that the previous night she had looked as if she might be getting well again, and when she left to deliver the pie early that morning, she had been much more "put together" than she had of late. By noon she had not returned home, and Fritz called the police. Later that afternoon, the police called back to report that Diana had taken her father's pistol, driven down a country road, and shot her self through the roof of her mouth.

We were all upset by Diana's suicide. Looking back, it seems surprising that the administration did not do more to help us deal with that tragedy. Fritz had been planning a move to an outpatient residency so he could start his psychoanalytic training. The timing of that was moved up, and in a few days he was gone. We did not get much of a chance to talk with Fritz, and we were left to mull things over on our own.

That episode led me to wonder about transference, counter transference and various other ways of categorizing love, such as the Greek's *philios* (abstract or brotherly love), *agape* (charity or compassion), and *eros* (erotic love). Did Fritz's love (*eros* as opposed to *agape*) for Diana cause him to delay her re-hospitalization? Did Diana's fear of how her relapse would affect her relationship with Fritz contribute to her suicide? Given an inexperienced therapist with such a difficult patient, would things have been different with closer supervision exercised more often than once every other week? It seems that suicide always leaves a lot of "what ifs" in its wake.

Technical considerations aside, suicide always disturbs me in a more personal way. I have always suspected that affective disorders (mania and depression) serve society when they do not get out of hand. Without them we would not have the creativity of the hypo-manics and the conscientiousness of the depressives. Then too, William James's[3] comment, "I hold no man mature until he has seriously considered self destruction," gives it a bit of a positive spin. But my grandfather committed suicide, and I saw what that did to his daughter and to his wife. And at least three members of my small medical school class killed themselves. So it is no great mystery why I find suicide threats distressing.

Part 3

Leaders of the Vision

40

Fabulous Phonies

I may have been carried away with the alliteration of the title, because I am not sure it is fair to say that Gregory Zilboorg and John Rosen were phonies. As with some other people who are privy to the revealed truth, details become trivial. A good example is Sir Cyrl Burt, who fudged his data on the genetic contribution to intelligence because the truth was obvious to him. So those gentlemen may perhaps be forgiven for behavior that seems reprehensible so long after the fact.

Zilboorg and Rosen have since largely disappeared from public awareness, but once upon a time they were hot items even in the lay press. Gregory Zilboorg was an authentic analyst and a thorough scholar. His *A History of Medical Psychology*[1] was required reading in preparation for the psychiatry board exams when I was a resident. He wrote numerous other books, including a translation of Paracelsus. He was also a brilliant speaker. I can remember sitting spellbound while I listened to him lecture. However, a colleague of mine once said his talks were like Chinese meals: you felt full just afterwards, but then felt empty a few hours later. In any event, his lectures were skillfully crafted and thoroughly memorized. Both then and now, psychoanalysts tend to read their papers at meetings. Modern empiricists project slides of hard evidence. They use their data as prompts, and if they try to read, attending to the slides makes them lose their place. In general, psychoanalysts do not have any data to use as memory prompts. Thus, they have trouble speaking from memory.

Zilboorg pretended to read his papers, but the fact that he had them memorized showed up on one occasion that I remember. He was to be the last speaker of the session. The other speakers had run overtime, so the chairman asked Zilboorg to cut his presentation short. Zilboorg replied haughtily, "Zo I vill read half of my paper!"

He proceeded to apparently read a page, take the next page, crumple it, throw it at the chairman, and so continue until he had finished a perfectly organized and elegant presentation; and used up his originally allotted time!

He was obviously gifted, but his self-promotion was outrageous. I have it on good authority that, during the Great Depression, he hired a beautiful, talented, but little-known actress to sail back and forth between New York and Europe on ocean liners. She rode first cabin, played bridge with the rich and famous, and from time to time let it be known that her apparent happiness—nay, even her beauty and talent at bridge—were the direct results of her analysis with Zilboorg.

He had a practice that included many famous people and became so well known that a funny-paper cartoon character was a psychoanalyst who was called Gregory Spellbound. Again, I have it on good authority that Zilboorg was analyzing George Gershwin for the difficulty Gershwin was experiencing in playing the piano with his left hand. He was dealing with the composer's masturbatory conflicts when the results of the right parietal brain tumor became even more obvious. By then the tumor was inoperable.

Of course, Zilboorg never came to Worcester. By the late 1940s he spoke for large fees, at high visibility meetings or when there were sources of rich referrals present. We could not fulfill any of those desiderata. But we did have a presentation by John Rosen. Rosen had been a pathologist, but after his personal analysis and a patient that (he claimed) he brought out of catatonic hyperthermia by making deep psychoanalytic interpretations, he became the prophet of what he called Direct Analysis. We residents worshiped Fromm-Reichmann, but her gentle and almost lapidary techniques were obviously not suited for the bulk of state hospital schizophrenics. In contrast, Rosen's papers were exciting, and a colleague had already experimented with his interpretation of Rosen's "Direct Analysis." He called his version, "An attack on the id from the rear." So Rothschild gave in to our requests, and we had a visit from Rosen just as he was beginning to be famous.

The case he picked for his demonstration was an out-of-control manic. Rosen had pulled in a fair audience, so he was on the stage of the big auditorium. The resident brought in the patient, who, seeing the audience, became even more flamboyant. He was talking a mile a minute, jumping up from his chair, sitting back down, and gesticulating broadly. Rosen sat on the edge of his seat, smoking a cigarette and listening attentively.

Abruptly, the patient reached into Rosen's shirt pocket, fetched the pack of cigarettes, took one, and then grabbed Rosen's cigarette to take a light from it. In the pause while the patient was drawing on his cigarette, Rosen said, "It's like touching two pricks together, is it not?"

The patient looked startled, but stood silently for a moment. Then he said, "Fuck you!" and burst into tears. Rosen gestured for the resident to take the patient away, saying "Now you have a depressed patient, and you can do psychotherapy with a depressive!" Rosen went on to explain that his remark had jolted the manic's underlying homosexual conflicts.

Since then, I have seen other manics switch abruptly into depression without any psychoanalytically based intervention. In addition, dysphoric (i.e., unhappy) mania is being recognized more frequently than it was even 10 years ago. But at the time, we residents were hugely impressed.

Rosen went on to describe his cure of a schizophrenic who had delusions of grandeur. He asked the patient to take him to an expensive restaurant, since the patient claimed to be so rich. The patient agreed. Rosen described how he had watched passively while the patient argued about the bill with the waiter. Then he had joined the patient washing dishes in the restaurant kitchen. After that, he claimed the patient had begun to work through his conflicts and to abandon his delusions.

Of all the residents, Irv Teplin was one of the more gifted therapists. He had a paranoid schizophrenic who seemed to be slowly regressing, and whose delusional system involved his belief that people were plotting against him because he was the world's greatest chess player. Now Irv had been a chess prodigy as a boy and was sure he could beat the patient. Rosen's tales of therapeutic progress after dramatically shocking patients and confronting them with the falsity of their delusions suggested to Irv a strategy for getting his patient to begin "reality testing." He would play the patient, checkmate him, and then gently get him to examine his beliefs. He played the patient and checkmated him easily, but the patient became mute and regressed even further.

Another of my colleagues took Rosen so literally that his attempt at direct analysis amounted to almost a *reductio ad absurdum*. He had a patient who claimed there were tiny machine gunners in the light bulbs, so one day the resident took a broom handle and broke all the light bulbs in the examining room. Then he said, "See. There are no machine gunners!"

The patient replied, "Of course not. You told them you were going to break the bulbs so they left!"

Did Rosen actually help any psychotic patients? I have a friend who worked for Rosen as surrogate "parent" and cared for one of his wealthy patients in a suite at the Plaza Hotel in New York. She remembers Rosen as a warm, totally dedicated person, and a loyal friend. She also knew a couple who worked for Rosen, and who claimed that Rosen had cured them of schizophrenia. But with the problems in telling manics from schizophrenics, and a 20 percent spontaneous remission rate in schizophrenia, who knows?

In any event, as time went on, so many of Rosen's ex-patients showed up in other psychiatrists' practices that there were demands for an investigation of his claims. One of my ex-fellow residents, Al Scheflen, who was by then a professor at an eastern university, took part in the inquiry. He had been favorably inclined toward Rosen, and was quite disappointed when he saw evidence of widespread deception by the father of

Direct Analysis. R.S. Bookhamer and co-workers[2] published a five-year follow-up of results of Rosen's patients in the *American Journal of Psychiatry*. They included some of Scheflen's data, and confirmed Scheflen's fears.

Are we any better today at weeding out phonies who make exaggerated or dishonest claims for non-drug treatments? The Federal Drug Administration (FDA) does a remarkable job of policing drugs and medical devices. By putting a stop to extravagant promises and demanding rigorous hypothesis-testing, they have put the days of the snake oil vendors behind us. Will we ever get the equivalent of the FDA for psychological interventions? In principle, there is no reason why not. People who talk of the subtleties and intangible factors in psychotherapy should take a look at the intangible factors in psychopharmacology. Admittedly, changes in psychological distress are a little more complicated to measure than changes in blood pressure. But they are, nonetheless, measurable with acceptable relevance and precision. While double-blind studies may not be appropriate, independent patient assignment and head-to-head comparisons with trained, monitored, "true-believer" therapists can give quite adequate results. So perhaps there will someday be a Federal Psychotherapy Administration.

41

The Psychoanalytic Innovator

The Worcester house staff embraced what they believed was cutting-edge psychoanalytic theory, vintage 1945, with a fervor that may be hard to believe now. The standard training trajectory was a couple of years at Worcester, then on to an outpatient-based residency in a larger city with a psychoanalytic institute where one could begin one's personal analysis. Such personal psychoanalysis was required by all of the psychoanalytic institutes before analytic training could begin. I was told that, once upon a time, Worcester allowed its residents to begin their personal analyses in Boston. Unfortunately, commuting to an analysis in Boston kept them away from the hospital so much that Rothschild stopped the practice.

Between celebrities visiting the Worcester Foundation and Dr. Rothschild's concern for our education, the residents were exposed to many of the great names of the day that came to consult at the hospital. In addition, when psychiatric luminaries came to Boston to speak, we drove in to attend their lectures. While most meetings of the Boston Psychoanalytic Society were closed to non-members, they occasionally had "open" meetings. When that happened, a group of Worcester residents usually drove in to attend.

I especially remember one open meeting of the Boston Psychoanalytic Society when a friend who had already begun his training analysis sat beside me and named off the famous personages as they arrived. To me, it was an impressive crowd, but the Deutsches stood out among the outstanding.

Helena Deutsch was famous for her book, *The Psychology of Women.*[3] It was first published in 1945, but today feminists would burn her in effigy. She, more than Freud, had argued for penis envy as the driving force in the female psyche. At the meeting, she strode in wrapped in a camel hair trench coat and towering above her husband, Felix, who was bald and sported a long cigarette holder.

Felix was not a favorite among Boston analysts because of a method of therapy that he had developed, which he called "Sector Analysis."

In those days, removing a symptom before it had been fully analyzed was supposed to cause the emergence of another symptomatic reflection of the underlying psychopathology. Felix Deutsch had declared that to be nonsense, and gave examples where people resolved a part of their problem in therapy, then had the rest of their psychopathology resolved by itself. Dr. Rothschild had great **regard** for Dr. Felix Deutsch, so he was invited to visit us and give a demonstration of his technique.

It was rumored that Felix Deutsch had been in the legitimate theater before medical school. In any case, he was certainly a showman. Before his visit, he had asked to have one of our most difficult patients brought for him to interview cold before our staff. Kay Cullinan, one of the residents, had a young woman patient who had made a serious suicide attempt. Now she did not seem seriously depressed, but she was so guarded that we did not trust her enough to let her go. Her family seemed benign enough, and nothing we could learn explained her serious attempt at self-destruction. Rothschild was afraid that behind her polite but frozen exterior was unseen turmoil that could lead to another suicide attempt.

In those days, one could keep a patient in the hospital purely on the basis of clinical intuition; that is, unless the patient had the sophistication to ask for a writ of habeas corpus. In such cases, a judge decided if the patient needed hospitalization, and the doctors usually were overridden. I'm sure the privilege of keeping someone hospitalized on the basis of clinical intuition could be abused, but that never happened at Worcester when I was there. Of course, people like Dr. Rothschild have never been in great supply, and I suspect there were other less benign institutions.

The celebrated Dr. Deutsch arrived early in the morning and began with a lecture on Sector Analysis. He spoke with the faintly British accents of a trained actor and with hardly a trace of his native German. Punctuating each point with the cigarette at the end of its long ivory holder, he explained how to listen for a clue that would allow one to focus in on the most pathological sector of the psyche. Next, he said, the trick was to focus on that sector until the patient came to recognize the nature of his problem. From then on, he said, it was a matter of listening and asking sensible questions. Anyone of reasonable ability, he said, could do that. Locating and uncovering the problem sector, however, was something that needed practice, talent, and perhaps a little luck.

Then Kay, the resident, gave a brief summary of the case. Deutsch had asked not to be told too much, but Rothschild had assured him that he need not worry. At the end of Kay's presentation, Deutsch beamed from ear to ear. When the young woman was brought in and introduced, he suddenly became a caricature of the Old World analyst. He kissed her hand, bowed her to her chair, and to our surprise began with a thick German accent. That, as he explained later, was useful when he wanted to focus on a sector by appearing not to understand something obvious.

"Undt zo, vat brinks you here?"

The patient began to tell her well-practiced and uninformative story. Deutsch listened with intense interest. When she stopped, he kept her talking with nods of the head and seemingly innocuous repetitions of words she had used. So far as we residents could tell, nothing much of interest was going on.

Then, in the course of responding to Deutsch, she made a remark about her mother followed by just the trace of a sarcastic expression. Deutsch suddenly sat up straight and raised his cigarette holder like a conductor calling a symphony to order. "Your mudzer?" he asked in a puzzled voice.

"Yes. Mother." she replied with a touch of irritation. "I was simply remarking how she tries to make everything look good."

"Bud your mudzer?" Deutsch persisted with a stage wink to the residents who were now on the edges of their chairs.

"She's a housewife!" the patient responded sarcastically. "You know, making pretty pictures is the most important thing."

"Ja. But vat es zis mudzer?"

"Mother. M-O-T-H-E-R, the one who should protect her daughter from her drunken father! You stupid Hun!" At that point, she dissolved into great heaving sobs, and Kay came forward to put her arm around the patient's shoulder.

Reverting to his clipped quasi-British accent, Deutsch said to the patient, "I believe you and Dr. Cullinan have some things to discuss." Then to Kay, he dramatically intoned the time-honored phrase by which anesthesiologists call surgeons to their work.

"Your patient, doctor!"

I am pleased to report that the case was resolved happily. Kay had to put up with some pretty wild outbursts of rage and one suicidal frenzy that required putting the patient in a "quiet room," the euphemism for a padded cell. But little by little things settled down, and the patient confronted her mother and then moved out. When last heard from, she was doing well in Manhattan.

Unfortunately, at the time it further reinforced our collective belief in the Freudian dictum that depression was always repressed hostility, and would resolve when the hostility could be expressed. I've seen only a few such cases since then. Two psychotherapeutic techniques for treating depression have now been tested experimentally and found effective. They are Cognitive Behavior Therapy and Interpersonal Psychotherapy. Neither of them particularly focuses on hostility, and I will comment on them later.

Sector Analysis went the way of most good ideas in psychology. It was assimilated, and pretty soon every one thought it had always been part of standard practice. Such movements as Rogerian Non-Directed

Psychotherapy once made much of focusing on salient problems, and that idea is alive and well in the protocols of modern Interpersonal Psychotherapy. So for most psychotherapists today, the practice of focusing (instead of encouraging free associations) seems so obvious as to be banal.

42

How Fortune Came to Favor the Foundation and the Hospital

Worcester's good luck began in 1921 and lasted through my time there at mid-century. First, the hospital enjoyed the reigns of two unusual administrators. Too often, administrators are limited and uncreative. Since research, teaching, and clinical practice are all usually more fun than administration, I suspect that those who fail at the more interesting occupations are the ones who gravitate to administration. Because of their limitations, they tend to emphasize the wrong things. It is truly a rare human being who has the talent, vision, and altruism to build, to facilitate, and to leave the hands-on fun to others while he or she juggles resources.

When teaching, research, and clinical practice are all of high quality; they tend to nourish each other. Unfortunately, it is a rare administrator who can allocate resources so that excellence in all three activities is possible. In fact, today as I write this, it is an even rarer medical administrator who has extra resources to allocate. When inadequate resources threaten survival, no administrative skill can ward off the resulting bitter infighting.

It is also rare for administrators not to use the authority of their positions to meddle with the operations in the field. I sometimes suspect that this meddling serves to bolster a self-esteem that has been damaged through failures in teaching, clinical practice, or research. Dr. William Bryan, surely one of the rare ones, was a truly visionary builder who served from 1921 to 1941. Dr. Bardwell Flower, who followed him from 1941 to 1969, did not meddle in the clinical, teaching, and research arenas, and so was, in his own way, special.

As we see in much of human history, chance also played a large part in what turned out to be the last renaissance in the cyclic history of Worcester State Mental Hospital. Worcester was started, back in the 1800s, as the international model for moral therapy. It then sunk into being a custodial care facility until, just before the start of the twentieth century, it blossomed again under Dr. Adolph Meyer as a center for the "psychobiological approach."

Once again it sunk into warehousing mediocrity until, with Bryant in charge, the first of the lucky breaks for what we can call "Worcester State Hospital's Twentieth Century Renaissance" came in the form of a grant from the McCormick Foundation. That grant is in itself an interesting story, and explains some of the inter-relations between the Worcester Foundation for Experimental Biology, the state hospital, the Schizophrenia Research Project, and (of all things) the development of the birth control pill.

Money comes in funny ways. In the case of the Worcester Foundation and the state hospital, they had schizophrenia to thank. Mrs. McCormick's husband, a grandson of the man who invented the reaping machine, had schizophrenia. A psychoanalyst treated him for years, and Mrs. McCormick felt he got worse as a result of the treatment. She decided to support biological research on schizophrenia with money from the McCormick Foundation. A number of Boston medical schools were vying for the McCormick money, but partly from their hubris and partly from the brilliance of Superintendent Bryant, the McCormick Schizophrenia Project ended up at the Worcester State Hospital. The project ran from 1924 to 1944 and began with a strong biological, almost anti-psychological, emphasis. Dr. Roy Hoskins, an eminent endocrinologist of the time, became director, and he quickly involved Hudson Hoagland and the physiology department of Clark University in the research.

Another lucky break for Worcester State was the failure of Hudson Hoagland to become professor of physiology at Harvard. It was around 1930 when Hoagland left Harvard to become professor of physiology at Clark University in Worcester. While that was not exactly a step up the academic ladder, such lateral arabesques are rather common career trajectories for Harvard professors, and Hoagland fully expected to return to Harvard as a full professor. But that return, and several other prestigious positions, seemed to have been snatched away from him at the last moment by academic politics over which he had no control. As a result, Hoagland stayed in Worcester and went on to make history as the co-director of the Worcester Foundation for Experimental Biology.

From the beginning, the visionary superintendent Dr. William Bryan and the Worcester State Hospital staff welcomed the intellectual contributions of Hoagland and his entire Clark University physiology group. The welcome was expressed by furnishing the Clark group with laboratory space in the hospital and involving them in research funded by the Schizophrenia Research Project. In 1934, Hoagland participated in the study of insulin shock treatment carried out by the Schizophrenia Project. In the late 1930s, he established the electroencephalographic (EEG) lab at the Worcester State Hospital, which functioned both as a clinical service and as a research resource for a variety of neurobiological investigations.

Dr. Gregory Pincus, a prominent endocrinologist, joined Hoagland on the Clark faculty in 1938. Hoagland and Pincus made a dynamic and charismatic team. Together they developed a stellar research-oriented physiology department that actually rubbed many Clark faculty members and administrators the wrong way. By getting extramural support, publishing important papers, and attracting talented students, Pincus and Hoagland managed to put enough noses out of joint that, by 1943, Clark had withdrawn all financial support for the physiology group, with the exception of Hoagland's tenured professorship. The other members of the Clark physiology department were forced to survive on meager grants and gifts, further diminished by university overhead, so Hoagland's decision to leave Clark and start the Worcester Foundation for Experimental Biology was not a difficult one.

Hoagland left Clark to launch the Foundation with Pincus as co-director in 1944, the same year the McCormick Schizophrenia Project ended. However, they retained the chemistry lab on the state hospital grounds. Fred Elmadjian was the foundation scientist who ran that lab. He lived in the hospital, and became one of my important mentors.

In 1945 they moved the part of their group that had remained at Clark to a beautiful country mansion in Shrewsbury. This was a picturesque village several miles east of Worcester, and incidentally, it was where Dorothy and I had lived when I first came to work at Worcester. The Worcester Foundation for Experimental Biology flourished in its odd but lovely Shrewsbury quarters and continued collaborating with the state hospital until 1968 when, flush with money from the contraceptive pill, the Foundation moved into new and elegantly designed buildings in the city of Worcester itself. But that is further along in this story than I mean to go now.

Curiously, the development of the contraceptive pill by the Worcester Foundation for Experimental Biology was closely related to the active collaboration between Mrs. McCormick's Schizophrenia Project in the State Hospital and the group of Clark University scientists that became the foundation.

The female's ovaries serve as endocrine glands. They excrete a number of steroid hormones that control the menstrual cycle and so determine when a woman can conceive. Endocrinology was then what molecular biology is today. It was hoped that endocrinology would shed light on mental illness. It was the original focus of the Schizophrenia Project and had always been Pincus's specialty. Not surprisingly, in 1951, Pincus and Chang began to develop steroids at the Worcester Foundation. It seemed plausible that some of these sex steroids might block human ovulation and so act as what we have come to call birth control pills. Mrs. McCormick knew of the work because of their association with the Schizophrenia Project. She introduced her friend, Dr. Margaret Sanger, to Pincus. Sanger was a famous birth control advocate, and when Pincus convinced the two women that he might be able to produce a birth control pill, Mrs. McCormick's foundation provided the money for the basic work. So Mrs. McCormick's interest in endocrinology paid off handsomely, but not in the treatment of schizophrenia.

Fortunately, Mrs. McCormick had also failed in her intention to keep psychology and psychoanalysis out of the Schizophrenia Project. I have not found an explanation for how the strictly physical approach to mental illness lost its grip, but somehow it did. In addition to a psychologist, David Shakow[4], being the last director of the Schizophrenia Project, the famous psychoanalyst Louis Hil, was one of the early project scientists and later became Director of Psychotherapy at the Sheppard and Enoch Pratt Hospital in Towson, Maryland.

In his memoirs, Hudson Hoagland[5] hinted that after Mr. McCormick died, Mrs. McCormick became much less involved with the research on schizophrenia that her foundation was supporting, so that more psychological approaches invaded the Project. Another possibility is that the biological studies were not bearing much fruit, while the more psychologically oriented approaches did turn up some hard data. This is not to say that the search for endocrine factors in mental illness stopped. I took part in several clinical studies involving endocrinology between 1948 and 1950, and I mentioned some of them earlier. But the sad fact was that hundreds of measurements were made during the Schizophrenia Project, but none of the endocrinological and other biological measures came close to the significance of the Phillips Scale, which was about as pure psychology as you can get. The blossoming of biological psychiatry was still a decade or more in the future.

The Phillips scale was based on clinical observations by Les Phillips, who became Chief Psychologist at Worcester at about the time I arrived. He had found that pre-psychotic psychosexual development predicts outcome in male schizophrenics. Phillips had derived his psychosexual development scores empirically from his studies of schizophrenics, although their theoretical underpinning came from psychoanalytic theory. At the lowest level and with the poorest prognosis were those real loners who had no relationships with other humans. Then came patients who had histories of transient relationships, with homosexuals scoring below heterosexuals. Next came enduring relationships, again with heterosexuals faring better than homosexuals. Next came marriage with divorce. A lasting marriage was given the highest rank. Curiously, such a ranking failed to predict outcome in female schizophrenics. Phillips speculated that some men marry women who are mentally ill when they are also attractive enough physically, while society affords males no such tolerance.

What I know of those years during the Schizophrenia Research Project is secondhand, but in my reading about the Project I encountered a level of sophistication that had, it seemed, never been applied before in the studies of the major psychoses. Efforts at making observations that could be repeated and that could be expressed in numbers were serious and sustained. They were guided by the latest developments in measurement theory (psychometrics) and employed advanced mathematical (multivariate statistical) methods of data analysis. The overall sophistication would be hard to match even today, although the calculations were done with hand crank Marchant calculators. (Few twenty-first century investigators appreciate how spoiled they are.)

What comes across the years, too, is a sense of camaraderie and purpose that fostered easy communication between psychologists, biologists, and clinicians. The members of the Schizophrenia Project clearly enjoyed the intimacy of living in the hospital, and a year after the Project formally closed, we still enjoyed the forced intimacy. The isolation afforded by the huge hospital grounds and meager distractions offered by Worcester itself allowed the staff to focus entirely on a task that was without a doubt both challenging and worthwhile. The ever-present mass of patients provided a counterpoint to the work, and was a constant reminder of the tasks that awaited us.

The first and greatest contribution made by the Schizophrenia Project was its documentation of ignorance. Before that time, most books and papers on schizophrenia had been written by single clinicians whose databases were naturally restricted. With a large population of cases, scrupulous observations, and careful measurements, it became clear that earlier authors had grossly oversimplified things. Certain clinical beliefs, such as the correlation between homosexuality and paranoia, had become urban myths, but many did not hold up under careful study.

Second, the research group found that on any of their measures, be they biochemical or behavioral, the range of values in patients diagnosed as schizophrenic was much greater than the range of values found in the normal people. This great variability among schizophrenics is a repeatable but puzzling observation that has long awaited a really satisfactory explanation. It is often put forward as evidence that the diagnosis of schizophrenia is made on patients suffering from any of a variety of poorly understood illnesses and does not define a unitary disorder. One commentator called it a "garbage pail" diagnosis. But today, molecular biology is beginning to identify some of the different genetic abnormalities that play roles in "the schizophrenias."

A third contribution was the extensive and careful study of insulin shock treatment mentioned above. Again, as is so commonly seen, glowing clinical reports lose luster when submitted to careful objective analysis. Insulin treatment did in fact seem to relieve some schizophrenics of their symptoms, but the benefits were often transient. In general, the value of insulin shock was much more disappointing than anyone had expected when the shock treatment was tested in a large scale clinical study with long term follow-up and with comparisons of matched treated subjects and untreated controls.

All the foregoing is to show that Worcester State Hospital from 1948 to 1950 was not an average state mental hospital. It explains the unusually well developed tradition of inquiry and scholarship I found there as well as the rich mix of mental health professionals and scientists who populate the stories I tell in *Asylum.*

43

From Madhouse to Mansion

From the hospital, the 10-minute drive across Lake Quinsigimon on the road to Shrewsbury would, before you reached the Shrewsbury town square, bring you to an elegant mansion set back on a green lawn, with a sign announcing that it was indeed the Worcester Foundation for Experimental Biology.

If Flower (superintendent) and Rothschild (clinical director) were the top dogs at the state hospital, their counterparts at the foundation were Hudson Hoagland and Gregory "Goody" Pincus, the co-director pair that I have already named. I have already described Hoagland, since he was my scientific role model. As far as I knew, he had no nickname. While Hoagland was a tall, trim, laid-back patrician, and usually puffed on a pipe in a professorial way, "Goody" was a stocky, intense scientist with a warm and humorous side. Both were brilliant, dedicated scientists, and they perfectly complemented each other. Hoagland was a renaissance man with a gift for raising money. "Goody" had the intense focus required of a successful investigator.

A year after the divorce from Clark, the Foundation had taken over a beautiful country estate in Shrewsbury that had belonged to the Hovey family. While the Foundation still had the one biochemistry lab at the hospital, most of the non-clinical research went on in Shrewsbury. There they were analyzing the chemical output of perfused adrenal glands, doing some chemical syntheses, and carrying out basic animal studies in neuroendocrinology. As its name suggests, neuroendocrinology was the relatively new field dealing with the interrelationships between the nervous system with its message-carrying neurons and those glands (endocrine) that secrete message-carrying chemicals into the blood (hormones).

Their Foundation laboratories occupied what must once have been an enormous banquet hall, with hardwood floors and French doors opening out to well-tended lawns. There was an air about the Foundation that suggested preparations for an elegant garden party. People were bustling about over the polished hardwood floors while spotless glassware glittered on tables, only the tables were lab benches with black acid-resistant tops, and the glassware consisted of retorts, fractionation columns, and the like.

The Foundation labs circa 1950 were quite odd, but really innovative research is often done in odd places. In their 1998 discussion of the history of genetics, Nobel Laureate Paul Berg and his colleague Maxine Singer[6] wrote:

> Looking over the past 150 fifty years—at the tiny garden at Brno, the filthy fly room at Columbia, the labs in the New York Botanical Garden, the basement lab at Stanford, and the sun-drenched early gatherings at Cold Spring Harbor—it seems that the fringes, not the mainstream, are the most promising places to discover revolutionary advances.

I was fortunate enough to visit both of the laboratories where Guiseppe Moruzzi and Horace W. Magoun did their pioneering work on the reticular formation, which is that part of the brain stem that plays a major role in controlling arousal, waking, and sleeping. Magoun's lab was in temporary military buildings at Long Beach, California, while Moruzzi's lab occupied a medieval structure in Pisa. Although the eleventh-century Italian architect could hardly have had that benefit in mind, the damping of vibration by the 20-foot-thick medieval walls may have had a lot to do with the precision of Moruzzi's early microelectrode studies.

I would not think of Moruzzi and Magoun as "fringe" neuroscientists any more than I would think of Berg and Singer as "fringe" molecular biologists, although it seems clear that important scientific advances often come nurtured in queer cradles. For my taste, the best explanation of the above phenomenon was described by H. Northcoat Parkinson[7] in his book on *Parkinson's Laws*. There he gives many other examples of great research work done in unsuitable buildings, and he offers a logical explanation. He suggests that putting scientists into perfectly designed structures constrains them to pursue the ideas held by the building's designers. By contrast, unsuitable buildings set them free to follow their own novel paths. Architects certainly make homes and offices better places in which to do routine things, but do they inadvertently put millstones around the necks of creative scientists?

In any event, the physical plants of the old hospital and of the old foundation never posed the slightest constraints on the imaginations of the investigators.

44

On Mink Mating and Money-Making

While I was at Worcester, I was never clear about the precise relationship between the Foundation and the State Hospital, but it appeared pretty relaxed. I do not recall any conflicts over turf, but of course, in those days, there was more than enough turf to go around. The world was not over-populated with either psychiatric residents or neuroscientists, and things were less formal in general.

I do not think I ever signed anything when I started my residency, nor did I get any certificate when I finished. At the start of my second year, I was told that I was a Foundation Fellow, but I never had anything in writing saying so, and my duties did not seem to change. Recently, I was asked to present all my diplomas and certificates to get hospital staff privileges. I do have a lovely diploma from Emory University saying I had completed my internship at Grady Hospital, and an elegant certificate stating that I passed my boards in neurology and psychiatry, but nothing else. I was hard pressed to prove I had ever done any residencies.

Apropos the casual collaborations between the hospital and the foundation, there was an amusing prelude to the ultimate development of the contraceptive pill. Almost from the beginning, the neuroendocrinological underpinnings of fertility had been one of the foundation's major scientific foci, whatever the scientific and economic motivations were. Funding was, of course, an ever-present concern. So it came to pass that someone thought of a way the research on estrous in minks might help make some money.

Until then, female minks came into heat naturally only once a year and had only a few pups. The reproductive physiologists figured that if they could make minks have three litters a year, they could triple mink production and so generate a nice income stream for the Foundation.

In due time the endocrinological chemists and physiologists succeeded in inducing estrous in female minks. However, cooperation from the male minks posed a problem. This came up at the hospital dinner table. Hearing the biologists complain, one of the hospital clinical psychologists with a background in animal psychology came to the rescue. He devised a female mink hand puppet that could be used to collect semen from male minks when the male minks were in the mood. Then the timing of the artificial insemination of female minks with induced estrous could be precisely controlled. With that, the foundation mink project was off and running.

Sad to say, the high price of ranch mink coats was in part due to the scarcity of mink pelts when minks copulated only once a year. The Foundation scientists did succeed in making minks bear three litters a year, but tripling the supply of ranch minks also drove down the price of mink pelts, and so the Foundation did not make the expected fortune. For that they had to wait until they learned to control human ovulation, and instead of getting mink ladies pregnant, they could keep human ladies from getting pregnant.

I am sure you can imagine how the hospital lunch table conversations were enlivened with tales of mink hand-puppets, mink-sex jokes, and fantasies of riches to come. But when the eventual crash of the mink market occurred, it was on to the next new idea.

45

Nate Kline

Just before I left Worcester, Dr. Sidney Sands departed to open a private practice in Des Moines, Iowa, and Dr. Nathan Kline came in as Director of Research. We overlapped only a few months, but that short time was enough for Nate to make a lasting impression on me. His dark hair, strong features, and general intensity reminded me of Leonard Bernstein.

He was incredibly energetic and overtly ambitious, but generous and willing to bring others along with him as he rushed to get ahead in the world. I was particularly taken by the contrast between Nate's unabashed desire to advance himself and the more gentlemanly postures taken by some of the New England Brahmins I knew. I say postures because I have seen plenty of evidence for driving ambitions behind the more aloof upper-class facades.

Nate was already recognized as something of a Renaissance man. He had a wide range of interests, and among his literary accomplishments was an English translation of Bleuler's classic German monograph on schizophrenia.

I particularly remember one time when Nate was taking off to a meeting in Boston. I think it was the Academy of Internal Medicine because I asked why he, a psychiatrist, was a member of such an organization. I wish I had paid more attention to his answer. He said in essence that it was a great way to make important contacts, advised me that who you knew was as important as what you knew, and invited me to come along with him. I did not take him up on his offer because at the time I did not think it would be worth the registration fee.

He quickly involved me in some studies he was doing on autonomic responsiveness in depression. On one occasion when I was serving as a "normal control," he gave me an injection that had been prepared by his assistant, so all Nate and I knew was that it was either a saline placebo or adrenaline. I had a brisk cardiovascular response, and was chagrined later when I found I had been given the placebo.

Nate went on in his uniquely flamboyant way to make medical headlines throughout his life. To his lasting credit, he recognized that when tubercular patients receiving isoniazide treatment became euphoric, it was not just the result of the improvement in their pulmonary status, but was also a true antidepressant effect. That observation paved the way for the development of the monoamine oxidase inhibitor antidepressants such as tranylcypromine (Parnate) and phenelzine (Nardil). Today those drugs are, because of some tricky side effects, underutilized by the current litigation-leery generation of psychiatrists. But they are still the most effective agents for certain kinds of depressed patients.

After Worcester, I saw Nate only at meetings, but from what I read he seems to have retained his wide ranging interests and his generous nature. In his book titled *The Serpent and the Rainbow*,[8] Wade Davis gives Nate considerable credit for helping him understand the puffer-fish poison, tetrodotoxin, which Davis claimed is used in the production of zombies by Haitian witch doctors. According to Davis, Haitian witch doctors scatter puffer-fish powder along with some abrasive on the floor, and when the bare-footed victim steps on it, he is turned into a zombie. Nate explained that the tedrodotoxin in the fish powder could be readily absorbed and would block sodium channels in nerve membranes. Nate said this could cause paralysis, temporary (hopefully) respiratory arrest, and brain damage. Davis took it from there.

Nate's style offended many people. I remember a time in later years when he arrived at a staid scientific meeting dressed in polished black boots and a riding habit. He walked up and down the aisle waving a copy of a book he had written and just had published. I would love to have a count of how many of the attending scientists he upset, and how many he delighted.

In his rush to get ahead, he also occasionally published findings that no one else could replicate. For example, he and his collaborators once claimed to have cured schizophrenia with beta-endorphin. He also was accused of over-enthusiastically prescribing psychotropic drugs, was sued for malpractice, and was vilified in the lay press as Dr. Feel Good.

I now suspect that Nate, like many geniuses, had a bipolar affective disorder (also known as manic depressive illness). Some of his behavior was clearly hypomanic, to say the least. Also, I certainly have to admit that sometimes Nate showed poor, or least unconventional, taste. But if those who criticized him made half as many contributions to the common good as Nate made, the world would be a vastly better place.

46

Marvelous Mentors

We all develop roles that we play repeatedly. We all get up in the morning, put our roles on, and zip them up like gorilla costumes. Then we go on autopilot and do not have to think about most of the transactions we have to make during the day. Various Gnostic disciplines go to great pains to help their disciples separate their "real" selves from the roles they play. However, for most of us, roles not only save us effort, they also embody our ideals and are indispensable. In other words, I do not think good roles are bad. While we develop our roles from family values, studies, and general experience, there are certain people that we imitate both consciously and unconsciously, and we can single them out as our role models. Two of my role models that particularly deserve honorable mention are Dr. Joe Wortis and Dr. Warren McCullough, and I will say a bit about each in the above order.

The first of the two actually sent me to work at Worcester, and thereby influenced the course of my entire life. Joe Wortis thus began to influence my life before I started my residency at Worcester and recommenced influencing me after I became an academic psychiatrist.

The way I chose Worcester was as follows. From as early as I can remember, I had assumed that I would go to medical school, do a surgical residency, and join my father's surgical practice in LaGrange, Georgia. But it had become harder and harder to ignore the fact that my hands were large and clumsy. In addition, I had a tremor that got worse when I tried to control it. Worst of all, I was finding the medical specialties more interesting and intellectually challenging than the surgical specialties. Among the various medical specialties, psychiatry and endocrinology seemed to be the most interesting to me. And so, some time during my last years as a student at Columbia University College of Physicians and Surgeons, I realized that I would never be a surgeon. Then, there was another factor. As a nephew of mine, who has marvelously dexterous hands, explained why he chose pediatrics over surgery, "Well, surgery is fun, but I couldn't stand the idea of spending the rest of my life with surgeons."

I think my father recognized that my decision to give up on surgery was best for all concerned. Most internships in those days were either medical or surgical, and we were both pleased when I was accepted for a medical internship at Grady Memorial Hospital in Atlanta.

I was considering both psychiatry and neuroendocrinology, and the thought of psychiatry as a potential specialty raised the issue of psychoanalytic training. For advice, I turned to one of my clinical professors who had taken a personal interest in me. He told me that endocrinology and psychiatry were both fields with promising futures. I told my professor that if I chose psychiatry, I did not know whether or not I should also pursue training in psychoanalysis.

"You should go talk to Joe Wortis," he had advised. "He lives in Brooklyn so he shouldn't be difficult to visit. He was analyzed by Sigmund Freud, but he also was the one who introduced insulin shock treatment to the United States."

Now, I knew that an analysis by Freud himself was an "open sesame" to the closed doors of the psychoanalytic institutes, while insulin shock treatment was the polar opposite of psychoanalysis. At that time, the biological "shock treatments" were anathema to the psychoanalysts.

My professor had continued, "He's about the only person I can think of that might give you an unbiased view on the subject."

So, after phoning for an appointment, I duly presented myself at Wortis's office in the basement of the Brooklyn brownstone where he lived. I remember it as a light, airy room that appeared both elegant and unpretentious at the same time.

I told Wortis that I was seeking his advice because my professor thought he would be unbiased regarding the pros and cons of psychoanalysis. To this day, I can clearly recall his response:

"Anyone who has significant experience with a discipline and claims to remain unbiased is either an idiot or a liar."

My memory of the remainder of the interview is understandably less exact, but I remember that he suggested I begin by seeing as many patients of different sorts as I could. He mentioned Worcester State Hospital as a good choice for such a beginning residency and also as a place where you could keep a foot in the door of endocrinology. So I followed his advice and went to Worcester, just like that.

I did not encounter Joe again until after my residency, but from that time on he had a profound influence on me. His *Fragment of an Analysis with Freud*[9] and his 1938 translation of Sakel's paper on insulin coma therapy established him as an intellectual colossus astride the two worlds of psychoanalysis and biological psychiatry long before the introduction of the psychotropic drugs.

Later, Joe, as I came to call him, was one of the leftists singled out by the McCarthy witch-hunt during the 1950s. While never a member of the

Communist Party, he knew many party members. He refused to co-operate with the committee by giving them the names of his friends. As a result, for a time he was stripped of his academic and governmental appointments.

After the McCarthy madness passed, Joe again assumed a leadership role in psychiatry and around 1969 helped found the journal, *Biological Psychiatry.* As its editor for almost a quarter of a century, he was a powerful voice for reason and progress in the field. When he founded the journal, there were few trained researchers in the field of mental health, so Joe used his editorial post as a bully pulpit for tutoring psychiatrists in good research practices. If a paper was submitted that had the slightest promise, he would encourage his reviewers to make detailed suggestions for revision, or even suggest experimental designs that would be more likely to result in a publishable paper. These days, most reviewers for scientific journals have neither the time nor the taste for teaching. Given the mass of research conducted and the volume of papers churned out, it is probably no longer appropriate or possible for editors to tutor the untutored.

During the time I knew him well, beginning some time in the 1960s and lasting until his death in 1995, Joe had more appointments and honors than he knew what to do with. Some sense of the man can be found in the 1996 collection of his editorials, *Psychiatric Tidbits.*[10] His writings reflect a man who had a continuing enthusiasm for life, for science, and for the art of psychiatry. He also had a delicious sense of humor and never seemed to take himself too seriously. He probably would not want an epitaph, and I certainly was not asked to write one, but I would have come up with something like *"Ethics before enrichment. Proof before plausibility."*

Dr. Warren McCullough, my other scientific role model, shared two great virtues with Dr. Joe Wortis: both were thoroughly devoted to learning, and both had enormously generous natures. Physically, however, they could not have been more different. Joe was compact and elegant, while Warren was rangy, bearded, and a member of what one of the University of California professors referred to as "the unwashed intellectuals."

It seemed that between the hospital and the foundation, almost every star in the fields of brain and behavior paid us a visit when I was at Worcester. Of course, in those days, there were not all that many stars in neuroscience. These great men would often meet at the hospital in the evening and speculate. In those days, everyone was searching for conceptual bridges between such things as neurochemistry, mathematics, computer science, and psychoanalysis. It was at one of those evening meetings that I first met Warren. He was striking to say the least, being about 6'4" with a red beard, and he reminded me of El Greco's "Christ." For someone with my ravenous curiosity, listening to any of the stars of neuroscience was a real privilege, but Warren McCulloch was and remains my personal favorite.

Warren's love of life and of his fellow man resulted in what I like to think of as benign hedonism. His research always had a play-like quality. Perhaps his most celebrated study is the one he and his co-workers published under the title, "What the Frog's Eye Tells the Frog's Brain."[11] Warren and his colleagues at MIT wondered if clicks and light flashes might not be inappropriate stimuli for the study of higher central nervous system neurons. In nature, frogs are especially concerned with flies, so they might be expected to have fly-detector neurons. And so, on exploring the frog's brain with microelectrodes, they indeed found neurons that became active (fired) only when there was a fly-like stimulus. Make the dot too small or too large, make its movement too fast or too slow, and the neuron fell silent. Building on those observations, the arch-reductionists David Hubel and Torstein Wiesel later won Nobel prizes in 1981.

I continued to seek out Warren, and must have had contact with him off and on for at least 40 years. He always seemed to be wearing the same rust brown suit, made of the finest tweed. He once told me that when it began to wear out he had it copied exactly. With only one suit, traveling was easy, and because of his brilliant mind, his facility with foreign languages, and his amiable disposition, he was welcomed warmly into the homes of prominent scientists around the world. Thus, the suit had been copied in many different countries. Of course he could never have had the suit cleaned, and I am not sure he ever bathed. For all that, however, he never smelled bad. I always suspected that his remarkable lack of body odor was related to the enormous amounts of alcohol he consumed. He never showed any sign of intoxication, so I suspect he was able to excrete alcohol in his sweat. Thus, perhaps he gave himself a continuous alcohol sponge bath.

I recall one occasion when he manifested both his legendary amiability and his legendary capacity for drink. One day in later years, when I had become a professor, I invited him to San Francisco as a visiting professor. I had also invited a psychoanalyst from Stanford who had written on computer simulation of psychoanalytic psychotherapy, and I had expected Warren to make mincemeat of the analyst. After all, Warren had written a hilarious parody of Freud's book *The Future of an Illusion*,[12] that he titled "Future of a Delusion." Parenthetically, I hope my continuing attempts to model myself after Warren have mitigated the inherent hostility behind my setting up what I thought would be a conflict.

Of course, Warren, the ever gentle scholar, found common ground with the analyst, and they ended up bosom buddies. When Warren's formal performance was over, the analyst and a gaggle of admiring students followed us to supper, where we drank and talked, and then on to a local bar called The Embers, where we drank and talked some more. At The Embers, the custom was for a bell to ring at a random time. If your glass was empty but still on the table when the bell rang, you got a free drink. There were four empty glasses when the bell rang, but their owners claimed they were not able to drink any more. So Warren asked the bartender, "Can I have four more Manhattans?"

"Sure" said the bartender and delivered the drinks forthwith. Warren continued his intense discussions until the Manhattans were completely gone and his audience was very nearly the same. Looking around at the glazed eyes of the remaining students, Warren graciously said, "Well, Noch, take me home and get me some coffee."

We drove to my house, and I made him a strong cup of coffee. While Warren drank his coffee, I went in to prepare the guestroom. When I came out I found Warren, fully clothed, sleeping on the floor. I woke him and suggested the bedroom. He replied, "I'm fine, Noch. I know where the john is. Just wake me when you get up."

The next morning, when I awakened him, he leapt to his feet and produced a pair of scissors with which he trimmed his beard. Then he launched into a discussion of how he had been dreaming about how the Fibonacci series ($N_i = N_{i-1} + N_{i-2}$; thus 0, 1, 1, 2, 3, 5, 8, 13, 21, 34, 55...) describes the arrangement of scales on a pinecone, and how he felt he now understood why that was true.

Warren was always warm, enthusiastic, and generous. On several occasions he gave me valuable help in criticizing my papers. I was told he died in his bed, well into his 70s, with a student's manuscript spread across his body. In a manner of speaking, he died with his intellectual boots on. What a way to go! His credo was a medieval Italian prayer that I can not quote in the original, but I remember the translation as follows:

"Oh God who loves me, teach me to love."

47

Consensual Validation: The Movie *Snake Pit*

In finishing my tales of Worcester State, I want to offer an independent view of what a "good" state hospital was like circa 1947. For such an independent view, I can think of no better source than the 1947 film *The Snake Pit*. It is truly a work of art, for it captures both the outer and inner realities of the time. First, it shows what it was like physically in a state hospital. Second, it accurately portrays the fantasy lives of the young idealistic staff physicians during the same period.

Olivia De Haviland plays a young matron named Virginia Cunningham. She is attractive, talented, and somewhat shy. Then, rather suddenly, she becomes psychotic and is admitted to a mental hospital. Her portrayal of an acute schizophrenic episode is entirely convincing. The setting is also incredibly realistic. The viewer sees intermediate wards with dormitory-like beds and day rooms filled with moderately intact patients. There is a back ward approached by a caged-in stairwell and filled with all sorts of disturbed patients. There are simple schizophrenics huddled on the floor muttering to themselves, and intrusive manics jabbering away at anyone handy. There are patients acting out their delusions like those in the Hogarth print of Bedlam.

There is a touching portrayal of a catatonic girl, standing like a statue but in obvious terror, who galvanizes into action and starts to strangle a manic patient who gets in her face. Fortunately at that point, Virginia Cunningham, who is on her way to recovery, intervenes and prevents the incipient tragedy.

While the building is off-putting, the grounds are pleasant. There is the "Open Pre-Discharge Ward" with its tiny private rooms. There is even the authoritarian and slightly sadistic head nurse.

In the course of her hospitalization, Virginia is given a short series of electroconvulsive treatments by her doctor "to establish contact." The procedure is shown with reasonable accuracy, although the shock machine looks much more formidable and elaborate than the one we used. The convulsion is not shown, but is hinted at by ominous and thunderous music. The movie received the Academy Award for sound recording. In the course of her treatment, Virginia is restrained in a "camisole" of the sort still in use today. She is even given a therapeutic bath by a hydrotherapist when she is wildly excited.

Staff meetings in *The Snake Pit* are also quite authentic. There is the table for the clinical director and ward chief, the comfortable chair for the patient, and the scattering of straight chairs for other physicians, nurses, social workers, and occupational therapists. Of course everybody smokes continuously. Even the staff dining room with the ongoing clinical arguments and discussions seemed familiar.

I found it somehow reassuring that Hollywood could actually treat the issue of mental illness with reasonable accuracy. But perhaps the reality of the old Snake Pits was so dramatic that no poetic license was needed.

Dr. Keck, *The Snake Pit's* psychiatrist, is the ideal of a young psychiatrist circa 1948, and plays a role we residents all fantasized for ourselves. He never has a hair out of place, and his suit is obviously expensive. He puffs

The Snake Pit. A still clip from the movie with Olivia DeHaviland as Virginia Cunningham and Leo Genn as Dr. Mark Kirk. On the wall we see Sigmund Freud as himself. *The Snake Pit* © 1948 Twentieth Century Fox. All rights reserved.

on a pipe and exudes an air of compassion, competence, and calm authority. He immediately senses that the patient has some buried trauma, and believes he can heal her if he can uncover her secret. In the film, every scene that shows Keck's office manages to pan past a large picture of Sigmund Freud hanging on the wall.

The psychiatrist-hero has not got much time for just listening, so he uses an Amytal interview as a way of blasting down to the patient's pay dirt. He quickly uncovers the fact that just before her beloved father had died, she had been angry with him for taking her mother's side against her in a family argument. Bingo! He tells her how this explains why she feared intimacy with males and why she had her psychotic breakdown when she got married. So she is cured, suffers no post-psychotic depression, and is filled with loving compassion for her fellow inmates who have yet to face their problems. In the final scene, she even has spontaneous insight into the fact that her love for her therapist was only transference.

It may sound absurd to present day readers, but the psychiatrist-hero is not too far off what we expected of ourselves. When I think back on the fruitless hours that I spent searching for offending memories like those found by the psychiatrist-hero, I must conclude I was a slow learner. But at the time I laid the blame on my own unanalyzed unconscious. I looked forward to the time when my own analysis would cause the scales to fall from my eyes, so that I could participate in such miracles.

Now, some 50 years later, I can recall a few non-psychotic patients where some rather specific repressed memory seemed to be the basis for repeated maladaptive behavior, and where the behavior changed when the memories were discussed. However, I have never seen a single schizophrenic whose illness appeared to result from a repressed conflict. Worst of all, I wonder how much my dogged and intrusive search for intra-psychic factors may have worsened and prolonged the psychoses of my patients.

48

Footnotes on Psychotherapy

Apropos of my remarks in the last chapter, I should confess that I began my own "personal" analysis just after I left Worcester. A personal analysis was (hopefully) a prerequisite to a subsequent "training analysis." I picked a Baltimore Psychoanalytic Institute analyst that Frieda From-Reichmann had recommended, and for two years I spent four hours a week on a couch. When my money finally ran out, I could not think of any brilliant insights that had come my way. I attributed that failure to my own inadequacies at the time, but now I am pretty certain that the fault was not entirely mine. So while I have come down pretty hard on the blind faith we had in psychoanalytic psychotherapy so long ago, a possible personal prejudice on my part should be taken into account.

However, I hasten to add that I am not against psychotherapy. A variety of psychotherapeutic procedures have been tried and found effective. Also, therapists who believe in any treatment (e.g., benzodiazepines for anxiety) have better results with that treatment than those who think the treatment will not work. So, I am not even against faith. However, what one takes on faith one should discard in the face of contrary empirical evidence.

In clinical practice, when faced with a sick person who is not responding to therapy "by the book," we are forced to improvise. When we see signs that our patient is getting better, one or another of our pet theories gets reinforced. Then it takes some effort to maintain our skepticism, and this is true both in psychopharmacology and psychotherapy. Testing hypotheses in psychotherapy can be daunting. Some types of psychotherapy are highly complex and difficult to test. Some take so long that no single therapist has experience with a sample of reasonable size. Yet, while the classical pharmacological double-blind often is not an appropriate model for testing psychotherapy, a variety of psychological interventions have in fact been adequately evaluated. There is a consensus that the best hopes for the mentally ill will lie in integrated social, psychological, and medical services, in having dedicated experts to provide those services, and in having unbiased evaluations of results.

Today, the mainstays of biological treatments for mental illness are our drugs, or what we call pharmacotherapies. Currently, the psychopharmacologist has a large number of highly specific agents with widely different profiles of desired effects and adverse reactions. Nevertheless, clinical psychopharmacology remains more an empirical art than a true science, as we try to recognize and capitalize on poorly understood differences among drugs.

Meanwhile, the general population has explored the actions of psychoactive drugs on its own, with disastrous results. For example, around 80 percent of chronic mental patients carry a "dual diagnosis," (e.g., they have both a mental illness and a drug addiction). The problem is not addressed by advertisements lumping all drugs together, as in the recent "War On Drugs." No one with a reasonable mind and a fair education is taken in by ads saying, "Drugs Fry Your Brain." Most teenagers know that Aspirin is not alcohol and marijuana is not cocaine. But honest education is hard to deliver in "sound bites."

Psychotherapy is even more bedeviled by mindless generalizations than is psychopharmacology. Even in sophisticated circles, psychotherapy often gets treated as if it were some sort of elastic head-band; one size fits all. This in part dates back to the psychoanalytic hegemony of the past, when all psychotherapy was either analysis or mini-analysis, and only lower level people without doctoral degrees, like social workers, concerned themselves with family interactions. By contrast, we can now call upon a variety of more or less specific psychological interventions, including special family, group, and social techniques. I will briefly review a few of the individual psychotherapies that have been thoroughly evaluated.

First, the idea that people need people seems to have been sufficiently tested in naturalistic and demographic studies. For mental health, and even for physical health, we must have friends with whom we can share experiences and feelings, and so check the reality of our conclusions. An interesting and relatively new discipline, derived from psychoanalytic thought, is attachment theory. It is now being used to examine some not so obvious physiological and psychological consequences of human relationships. So the most elementary, and perhaps most ubiquitous, feature of psychotherapy might be called the "rent-a-friend" business.

Closely related to the "rent-a-friend," but vastly more potent, is the "shared task" phenomenon. The shared task effect occurs when a person participates with a leader in an extremely demanding task, one that both of them perceive as valuable and well worth the effort. This is probably a factor in all the other psychotherapies to be considered below. It may account for life-changing encounters with gifted teachers and for the apparently inexplicable involvement of otherwise intelligent individuals with bizarre cults and religions. All of us probably carry some primitive longing for an all-powerful parent-teacher. Sharing a task, an idea, a job, or a movement with a leader can generate a psychological force that far outweighs the apparent power of the initial mutual interest.

Then there are the more or less direct offsprings of B. F. Skinner, known collectively as behavior therapies. Animals, including humans and rats, repeat behavior that is rewarding or positively reinforcing, and they avoid behavior that is punishing or negatively reinforcing. Those behaviors are called conditioned responses, because they depend on the conditions of reinforcement, and they disappear (e.g., become extinguished) if the reinforcement stops. For just one example, if there is panic every time a phobic patient confronts the feared situation, this negative experience reinforces the need to avoid the panic-inducing situation. Panic attacks are most likely to occur in crowds, and so agoraphobia (*Agora* = marketplace in Greek) is a common co-morbidity with panic disorder. If the patient can be taught to relax and approach the phobic situation in tiny, non-panic-inducing steps, such as can be achieved by directed fantasy, the phobic terror can be extinguished. While this approach really works, systematic desensitization, as this therapy is called, is so painfully boring for the therapist that it conditions most therapists to avoid it.

A sort of hybrid offspring of psychoanalysis and behavior therapy is called "Cognitive-Behavior Therapy"[13] or CBT, and it has been shown to be as effective as antidepressant drugs in some forms of depression. In the cognitive part, patients rationally examine faulty belief systems (i.e., I am no good). In the behavioral part of the anti-depressant version, they learn to replace the depressive's habitual self-hate cycle of (1) impossible expectations, (2) failure, and (3) punishment, with the self–healing cycle of (1) reasonable expectations, (2) success, and (3) reward. While I have oversimplified outrageously, this powerful approach is really not that much more complicated. More recently, a modified variety of Cognitive-Behavior Therapy has been developed for various anxiety disorders, and a specialized technique called Dialectical Cognitive Behavioral Therapy has been shown to be effective in borderline personality disorders.

There is "Interpersonal Therapy"[14] or IPT. Again to oversimplify, the actions of the therapist are not too different from those of the good listener who inquires about a friend's behavior in detail and questions whether there might be alternatives to behaviors that had undesired results. However, strict protocols for IPT have been developed to use in research, with other psychotherapies serving as controls. As a result, the effectiveness of this approach has been demonstrated in approximations of the double-blind trials that are required before the Food and Drug Administration will approve a drug. And IPT is certainly more interesting for the therapist than is behavior therapy.

The psychological treatment of choice for post traumatic stress disorder (PTSD) is "Eye Movement Desensitization and Reintegration"[15] or EMDR. Early on, heated controversies generated extensive experimental evaluations, because the results of EMDR were dramatic but counterintuitive. For example, therapists generally played the roles of passive observers to the changing experiences of patients, yet psychological material got worked through in hours, where with other methods it would have taken months.

PTSD patients usually recall minute sensory and motor details of traumatic experiences, as though these painful recollections had been immune to time or reason. These amazingly fresh and persistent memories continue to negatively influence a person's self-evaluation, and to generally interfere with healthy functioning.

Over-simplifying as before, EMDR employs cycles of experiencing, distraction, and reporting. The patient is asked to re-experience something distressing about the traumatic experience, the therapist interrupts or distracts the patient from the re-experiencing for about a minute, and then the therapist inquires about the patient's immediate experience. The therapist then says something like, "Let's go with that," and the cycles of distraction and inquiry are repeated until (among other things) the post-distraction experiences stop changing. Distraction was originally accomplished by having the patient move his eyes from side to side, hence the term Eye Movement Desensitization. Since then, other physical distractions have also been found to work quite well.

I also must confess to a prejudice in favor of EMDR because of a positive personal experience as a patient, followed by several positive experiences as a therapist.

Last (although they should in some sense be first) there are the "dynamic psychotherapies" that try to provide patients with insights into the machinery or dynamics behind their behavior. They are the most fun for therapists. These therapies come in more flavors than Baskin Robbins ice cream. Examples include Freudian, Jungian, Sullivanian, Adlerian, Ericksonian, Bernian, and so on. Some postulate infantile conflicts, some believe in working with psychological archetypes, some are concerned with the struggle for power, etc. Usually they involve great psychological and emotional investments from both therapist and patient. All are based on the dubious assumption that if you knew what motivated your sick behavior, you could stop it. Do insight therapies produce any more positive results more than would be expected from the shared demanding task phenomenon? That remains to be demonstrated. Certainly there are many ex-analysands who have gained insight into the dynamics of some portion of their undesirable behaviors, while the behaviors in question remain solidly unmodified. Most psychoanalysts call this "intellectual insight."

But putting aside my prejudices as best I can and venturing into some unfamiliar territory, I found several psychoanalytic groups that are hard at work trying to tease useful and testable hypotheses from more or less classical Freudian analytical theory. The fruits of this work by one group founded by Joe Weiss (the San Francisco Psychoanalytic Research Group, see www.sfprg.org) are illustrated in a paper by Marshal Rush and Suzanne Gassner[16] that I quote below:

> The research design was as follows. One group of judges were given the control-mastery plan formulation for the termination phase of the treatment and asked to rate the analyst's termination interpretations on the dimension of plan compatibility, i.e., how much the intervention contradicted or supported Mrs. C.'s pathogenic beliefs. An independent group of raters evaluated the patient's attitude towards termination preceding and follow- ing each intervention to see how that attitude was affected by the interpreta- tion. This group was unaware of the content of the interpretations. Each group of raters achieved high reliabilities, indicated good agreement between them.
>
> We found a highly significant correlation between how pro-plan the analyst's interventions were and how much the patient, immediately following these interventions, showed an increase or decrease in her resistance to the idea of termination. Pro-plan interpretations were associ- ated with immediate decreases in the patient's resistance to termination, whereas anti-plan interpretations were associated with immediate increases.

I cannot think of a better summary of what is required in modern Science (with a capital S) than the 2001 commentary by Edmonds` and Eidnow[17] on Sir Karl Popper's 1945 *Open Society and Its Enemies:*[18]

> Attack authoritarianism, dogma, and historical inevitability; stress toler- ance, transparency and debate; embrace of trial-and-error; distrust certainty; and espouse humility.

So, on the basis of the above and similar efforts, I must admit that psychoanalysts are beginning to do "Real Science"

Those of us in the field of mental health are moving eagerly into the twenty-first century. We have an enviable array of interventions, psycho- logical as well as pharmacological, that have been carefully tested. They have shown efficacy (i.e., they work), and they do not have unacceptable associated adverse events (i.e., do not cause problems that outweigh their benefits). To top all that off, exciting new interventions are presently undergoing evaluation, while entirely unexpected discoveries can be con- fidently predicted. But we will never be able to stop testing our ideas against the real world, and in ways that will tell us when we are wrong.

Part 4

It's Only the Castle Burning

49

Welcome to the Third Millenium

In 1947, Dr. Paul Beeson was Professor of Medicine at Emory University, and Chief of Medicine at Grady Hospital. I was a medical intern there. One day, towards the end of my internship, Beeson called me in to discuss what I wanted to do for my next year. He had a low-slung canvas chair in his lab where he used to relax. When I told him that I had decided on a psychiatric residency after my medical internship, he literally fell out of his chair onto the floor.

Getting up and sliding back into his chair, he exclaimed, "Callaway, you're a good doctor. You don't have to go into psychiatry!"

In the same vein, I remember my surgeon-father telling me this "joke" when he learned I was going into psychiatry:

It seems a young male psychiatrist attended the annual meeting of the American Psychiatric Association and fell hopelessly in love with a young lady psychiatrist. Their torrid love affair was put on hold while they returned to their respective practices, and as soon as the young man got caught up with the backlog caused by his vacation, he began calling and writing his loved one, but to no avail. He attended the next psychiatric annual meeting hoping she would be there but was disappointed again. Two years after the first romance-filled meeting, he attended another one and there she was again. He was somewhat cautious, but she embraced him with great affection.

"Where have you been the past 19 months?" he asked.

"Having a baby," she said.

"Mine?" he asked.

She nodded.

"Why didn't you let me know? I love you and would have married you!" he exclaimed.

"Well," she said, "My father is a surgeon and he said he'd rather have a bastard in the family than another psychiatrist."

But eventually psychiatry got a better cachet, and 20 years later, my dear surgeon-father was writing papers on the psychological issues involved in caring for terminal cancer patients!

I hope the preceding chapters have conveyed some feeling for state hospital psychiatry around 1948. By the same token, I intend the vignettes recounted above to convey a feeling for the prestige (or lack thereof) enjoyed by psychiatry in those days. Now, for those readers outside the field of mental health, I will tell a few more stories to give some feeling for the way psychiatry and the field of mental health is today.

First, the quality and quantity of people in the field have increased exponentially. Simultaneously, both as cause and effect, the field has become, socially and economically, much more rewarding. Take the American College of Neuropsychopharmacology (ACNP) meeting of 1997. The ACNP is one of the most prestigious societies for mental health researchers, and drug company money helps make the meetings elegant as well as informative. Dave Braff, a former student, was a Professor at the University of California San Diego (UCSD) and one of the top research psychiatrists in the country. He suggested we get together with our wives for cocktails, saying that there was something he wanted to discuss with me. I could not help remembering when a much younger and less eminent Dr. Braff had his first application for membership in the ACNP turned down. On that occasion, he had dubbed the organization "The American College of Narcissistic Pharmacologists." Now he was a Fellow of the College, highly important, and much sought after. Happily, his sense of humor, including his disinclination to take himself too seriously, seemed undiminished.

The ACNP was meeting on the Big Island in Hawaii at the luxurious Hilton Waikoloa Village. We were to have cocktails at the Kamuela Provision Company restaurant, which was located on the west side of the "village" complex, high on a pile of volcanic rock. From there, Dave promised, we would be able to see the "green flash" at sunset, the visual aftereffect produced the moment the sun sets below the sea on a clear evening. When the red glow of the setting sun is abruptly cut off by the sun's final drop below the horizon, an apparent flash of green light replaces the disappearing edge of the sun.

The Society reeked of prestige. Three Nobel laureates and the top neuropharmacological researchers from around the world were at the meeting. The afternoon before our cocktail engagement, I had been at a panel session listening to Bob Friedman from Denver deliver a dazzlingly brilliant paper on the genetics of schizophrenia. Supported by large grants from the National Institute of Mental Health, Bob had studied animals and humans with techniques as diverse as electrophysiology, genetic analysis, and molecular biology, to discover a gene for one of the acetylcholine receptors that might be a player in the development of schizophrenia. Acetylcholine is a neurotransmitter that plays many roles throughout the brain, and an abnormal form of one acetylcholine receptor seemed to be a "permissive" factor in the development of schizophrenia.

That is to say, the genetic abnormality does not cause a person to have schizophrenia, but when combined with other factors, it allows the symptoms to manifest themselves. Bob's work was also an example of modern "interdisciplinary" research. He called on a variety of experts for help with their specific technologies, but not to brainstorm in search of overriding general principles. In broadest terms, they developed hypotheses, preferably more than one at a time, and then tested them so as to discard the false ones. With my usual optimism, I wondered if the identification of this permissive gene might be the first truly basic theoretical advance in understanding the biology of schizophrenia.

Dave and his wife, Sandy, were waiting at the restaurant when Dorothy and I arrived. After we ordered our drinks, Dave came right to the point with me. He explained that, as President-elect of the Society of Biological Psychiatry, he was faced with a movement to change the name of that organization. Many of the younger members felt that the name was meaningless, as now there was really no psychiatry other than biological. He wanted to know how I, as a representative of the "old timers," would react to a name change, and what alternative names I would suggest. I agreed that the name of that society was indeed an anachronism, although I said that anachronistic names for journals and organizations are not necessarily bad. The prestigious English medical journal called the *Lancet* is an example. But if change was required, I suggested "The Society for Investigative Psychiatry," since an organization called the Psychiatric Research Society was already in existence.

50 years ago, about half the stars in neuroscience could fit into the small conference room at Worcester. In 1997, the prestigious crowd at the ACNP was a select sample from the huge cadre of research clinicians and brain scientists who now enjoyed enormous (but never enough) financial backing from government and industry, and who produced new discoveries at an ever-increasing rate. The growth of biological psychiatry as exemplified by the ACNP also illustrates how things have changed from the days when Freudian psychoanalysis was the dominant force in psychiatry.

Of course, Freud's personal experience with cocaine had taught him that drugs can alter the mind, and in his *Projects for a Scientific Psychology*,[1] he had prophesied that chemicals would eventually provide the best treatments for mental disorders. I wonder if he would have been surprised by just how true his prediction turned out to be. Some zealots claimed that only one who had completed a personal analysis could evaluate their pronouncements, which was hardly an invitation to open critical evaluations. In many of their explanations of mental phenomena, plausibility took the place of scientific proof. Their psychodynamic formulations captured the minds of many in the arts and letters, and are indeed appealing. For example, the character traits of tidiness, punctuality, and stinginess are in fact curiously associated. Freudians plausibly explained that association on the basis of conflicts during "anal" development. They argued that issues of cleanliness, timing, and a latent desire to hang on to one's excrement (stinginess) all came into prominence during toilet training, when the child was preoccupied with anal sphincter control. Subsequent studies have, however, failed to reveal any evidence for the hypothesized connection. For example, children born with congenital defects that include the absence of anal sphincters still may show "anal" traits as adults.

In any case, since 1997, biological psychiatry has taken over. Psychotherapies are being scientifically evaluated, new drugs are being delivered with increasing frequency, neuroscience leaps ahead, and the "evidence-based" practice of psychiatry is all the rage. Of course, science has its limits. After all, the polio virus is alive and well in Africa. And how far has the United States really come towards solving the problems of mental illness?

50

Visits With Those Left Behind

I retired in 1994, continued to practice charity psychopharmacology for about 10 years, and then found that I could no longer give my services away. Happily, I found I was much sought after by contract psychiatric service providers who insisted on paying me. So I continued to enjoy working with patients and applying the latest advances in psychiatry. I also came to know a variety of clinical settings.

But around 1999, before contract work expanded my horizons, I became aware that things were not all going well in psychiatry at large. That year, I got an invitation to attend the "End of the Trail" dinner given by the Napa (California) State Hospital psychiatric residency training program.

Before Governor Reagan decided that mental illness was a myth, Napa State Hospital had its own research department. In those days, the scientists at Napa State and those of us at UCSF visited back and forth, so I came to know Napa State well. Even after the research department closed, I continued to visit and teach residents. It was as an emeritus residency instructor that I was invited to the "End of the Trail" wake for the passing of the Napa residency training program. For a residency program to be approved, there have to be enough new admissions, and a sufficient variety of psychiatric disorders to afford the trainees a broad enough clinical experience. With the criminalization of the mentally ill, most of the hospital had been turned into a forensic (i.e., criminal) facility. And so, the civil part of Napa State Hospital, where non-criminal patients were kept for medical reasons, had shrunk to such a husk of its former self that it could no longer furnish the breadth of clinical experience required for an approved residency in psychiatry.

In talking with my colleagues at the wake, I realized how ignorant I was about the plight of patients of the sort I had treated at Worcester half a century before. Although I had read a bit about the criminalization of the mentally ill, I realized I did not have much firsthand experience with the issue. So I got Ed Brennon, director of the now defunct residency program, to arrange a tour of Napa State Hospital for me.

Driving up from the San Francisco Bay Area, I thought back to the lush green of New England as I went through the golden hills of the Sonoma and Napa valleys. I looked with amazement at the wall-to-wall vineyards and magnificent wine chateaux that had sprung up since my last trip some eight years earlier.

From the outside, Napa State looked unchanged. The divider for the main drive was still lined with stately old magnolias. The grand trees and the well-kept lawns looked the way they did 15 years ago, although I noted that the tennis courts had fallen into ruin. Behind the hospital, the land that had once been the hospital farm lay fallow. Rolling hills of golden grass dotted with stands of pin oaks contrasted with the deep blue sky. I parked on the main drive and walked around the administration building to Ed Brennan's office in the education building. After half a cup of coffee and a few minutes of small talk, Ed swept me off for a tightly scheduled four-hour morning. I came home with an armload of notes, a book, and some unsettling thoughts.

In the hospital, I saw only one patient wandering around. Most were occupied with group meetings and such. When I commented on the cleanliness of the ward, and the obvious attempts to engage all patients in group activities, I was told that some of those amenities were due to the state-mandated ward staff/patient ratio, which was 1 to 8 in the day-time and 1 to 16 at night. However, everything smelled so clean and looked so well kept that I wondered if it could be due just to the numbers of nurses and attendants, and I suspected that the clean, odorless wards were also due to two other factors. First, a static patient population is much cheaper to handle and easier to keep clean than is one with a rapid turnover. Second, I suspected that the absence of odor was because brain-damaged patients (as opposed to schizophrenics) made up such a large percentage of the new state hospital population. It is not that I longed for the old smell, but I suspected its absence told another story.

When I asked what had happened to the new admissions, my introduction to the criminalization of the mentally ill began in earnest. I was told that, in the past, the police would bring obviously mentally ill patients to the hospital, but since then, new regulations governing state hospital admissions (designed to guard patient's rights) required them to spend half a day doing paperwork, so they simply took the psychotic individuals to jail.

In the last of the three wards in the civil hospital that I visited, the staff physician there handed me a copy of *Madness in the Streets*, published by R.J. Isaac and V.C. Armant[2]. I saw that she kept a stack of the books handy. That book is such a detailed indictment of the deinstitutionalization, and subsequent criminalization, of the mentally ill that I will return to it in the next section. Supplementing the material in the book with some of her own experiences, she told me how, in California, the new determinate sentences spill untreated insane prisoners out onto the streets at the end of their incarcerations without any adequate follow-up care. Thus, if people with schizophrenia are convicted of crimes and do not plead insanity as a defense, they receive determinate sentences to prison, cannot be given drugs in prison without their consent, and, once their sentences are served, they are simply turned back out on the streets.

She told of a family that could only get treatment for a psychotic son by having him arrested for stealing food from his grandparents. Then they convinced him to plead "Not Guilty by Reason of Insanity," also known as NGI. Otherwise, as a civil commitment, he could not be held unless "an immediate danger to himself or others," and in any case he could not be treated without his informed consent. Apparently, if one pleads NGI, the need for treatment is established and the patient loses the right to refuse medication and the right to use street drugs.

Next came my biggest surprise of all. Leaving the remnants of the civil hospital, we walked across the bucolic campus to the forensic facility. "Forensic" comes from the same Latin root as forum, and has to do with the courts of law. Thus, "forensic facility" is a euphemism for "hospital for the criminally insane." It was hidden behind a forbidding razor wire fence with a guard station set into it. Ed Brennan had gotten permission for me to visit, so I presented myself, turned in my driver's license, received a visitor's badge, and was passed through heavy security.

We entered a busy, pleasant hospital. Patients garbed in crisp tan uniforms were engaged in animated conversations, and while I was there, a jolly group departed for an outing in the wine country. The staff psychiatrist in charge of the forensic unit must have seen my mouth fall open, for he said, "I guess you noticed that my forensic patients are much healthier and less crazy than other psychotic patients."

He explained that about 85 percent of the patients in Napa State Hospital, whether civil or forensic, had dual-diagnoses, one for a mental illness and the other for a substance abuse. Substance abusers usually have to be detoxified and then kept clean and sober before effective treatments of their mental illnesses are possible. This was usually feasible only for the forensic patients, because in most cases the control of psychotic, drug-abusing patients requires a locked facility with tight security as well as involuntary medication. But, given those requirements, the success rates were impressive.

I asked if marijuana was one of the abused substances, and the staff psychiatrist laughed. He said that there was one patient whose problem was "pot," but he was in trouble more for farming it than smoking it.

Finally, I asked about teaching and research. While the once proud state hospital no longer had students or research projects, the forensic facility had close ties to the medical school at University of California Davis and collaborated with them both in teaching and in research.

I am afraid, even now in 2007, that the psychotic individual who commits a felony and pleads not guilty by reason of insanity is indeed fortunate!

But not all of the patients we cared for at Worcester were schizophrenics. There were also manics, depressives, obsessive-compulsives, borderline individuals, various toxic reactions, etc. I knew that many of these sorts of cases were served by local mental health clinics and acute psychiatric emergency facilities associated with general hospitals. Those that needed longer care in a locked facility were sent on to so-called "L" facilities. As part of deinstitutionalization and the closing of big state mental hospitals, each county was supposed to have such a low-cost mini-mental hospital so that patients needing continuing hospital care could be treated nearer to their homes. But my newly aroused curiosity was no longer so easily satisfied. I decided to visit Canyon Manner, my own Marin County's "L" facility in Novato, California, and obtained an invitation from its medical director.

Early one morning in 1999, I drove 20 miles north to search for Canyon Manor. I guess I had some preconceived ideas about the physical plant, because I drove by the building three times before I stopped a passing pedestrian and had it pointed it out to me. It turned out that the title "Canyon Manor" referred to its street address rather than to the nature of the facility itself. The "L" facility turned out to be an unimpressive one-story complex laid out in the shape of an H, and surrounded by an inconspicuous fence. What with its patios and exercise areas, I had taken it for an elementary school. On close examination, I could see that there were locked gates in the honeysuckle-covered fence, but the fence itself was not designed to deter a determined and reasonably agile individual from leaving.

My tour was informative, and a description of that "L" facility visit once occupied a long chapter in an earlier version of this book. Here are two observations that seem worth salvaging. First, the old familiar smell of chronic schizophrenia (the one I missed in the state hospital) was alive and well at Canyon Manor. There are some chronic schizophrenics who are not in jail or on the streets. Second, while Canyon Manor had no students, no research programs, and few specialized facilities, I have to admit that, advances in psychopharmacology aside, I would rather be a patient at Canyon Manor in 1999 than a patient at Worcester State in 1949.

In closing this chapter, I cannot resist making a few remarks about California's politics. First, under Governor Edmund "Pat" Brown (1959-1967), mental health enjoyed a level of support that it had never seen before, and may never see again. For example, around 1960, it became apparent that the plan for a research division in every state hospital was overly ambitious. Leon Epstein, then Director of Research for the California Department of Mental Hygiene, went to the legislature and asked them not to give him more money because he could not find enough qualified people to staff the positions he already had.

When Ronald Reagan became governor of California in 1967, he subscribed to the idea that mental illness was mostly a myth. He promptly gutted the Department of Mental Health, and shut down the state hospital research operations that had been built up under Brown. I find it ironic, if not poetic justice, that Ronald Reagan eventually died from Alzheimer's dementia.

In 2001, California had a proposition on the ballot that would substitute outpatient treatment for prison time in convictions for nonviolent drug possession. The proposition passed by a wide margin, in spite of the fact that the Correctional Officers Association (prison guards) was lobbying against it. However, our revolving door penal system spins on, and looks like it will maintain the demand for correctional officers for many years to come.

51

Are Promises Made To Be Broken?

In a sense, we seem to have come full circle. The original intent of Worcester (as the Worcester Lunatic Asylum) was to put a stop to the criminalization of the mentally ill. Now it seems that modern scientific psychiatry is in a race against those who, once again, would imprison and mistreat the mentally ill. So let us look again at history.

Before 1991, Worcester State Hospital had suffered years of terminal neglect. Its death and cremation in 1991 offers an almost irresistible metaphor. One thinks back 157 years earlier to the time when it was born and named The Worcester Lunatic Asylum. It was the first state hospital for the mentally ill in the United States. It presaged or mirrored the history of how America has treated its mentally ill for the last 185. Its immolation was a symbol of deinstitutionalization.

The Worcester Lunatic Asylum began largely as the result of efforts by Horace Mann to introduce the "Moral Treatment" of the mentally ill. It was a time when reason and compassion, persistently and firmly applied, promised to supply answers to most of the world's problems. The term "Moral Treatment" was the embodiment of this philosophy. It was obviously irrational to treat mentally ill individuals as criminals (or so it seemed in the 1830s), therefore "insane" (i.e., mentally unhealthy) individuals were moved from prisons to hospitals. This was a remarkable moment in the history of mankind's efforts at being humane.

The lunatic asylum's first superintendent, Samuel Woodward, was also a visionary reformer like Mann, and both were actively supported by other reformers of their era. I remember a picture of patients at Worcester Lunatic Asylum having a lawn party around 1840. They are elegantly dressed, and the women have parasols. The whole thing looks quite upper middle class.

However, even as Worcester Lunatic Asylum was being imitated in most of the other states and being hailed as a model by reformers like Dorothea Dix, it was beginning to fall short of its founders' dreams, although through no fault of its own. Time had changed the rules of the game. Industrialization and the influx of immigrants to New England overwhelmed the institution with people whose culture and language did not equip them to benefit from large doses of white, Anglo-Saxon, Protestant values. One can just imagine a New England Protestant physician, with the stiff white collar of the time, trying to apply "Moral Treatment" to a non-English-speaking Catholic immigrant woman from Italy, who lacked finances and community support to leave the hospital, even if she could comprehend what her doctor was trying to accomplish.

So the enthusiasm of the founders did not survive to the next generation, and by 1877 the function of the hospital had already become more custodial than therapeutic. That year, the enormous and forbidding fortress that I knew in 1948 was built to supplement the original hospital. Was the fortress-prison designed to protect the insane from the public, or vice versa?

Meanwhile, medicine was making advances by relating physical pathology to clinical disease. Excessive sweet urine (diabetes mellitus) was related to changes in the pancreas, while excessively watery urine (diabetes isipidus) was related to changes in the pituitary. The courses of infectious diseases were being related to specific microorganisms, and so on. Psychiatry tried to follow suit. However, since there was usually no observable physical pathology to correlate with psychiatric symptoms, faith in the physical cause of insanity remained just a faith. Faith can be a good thing, but hope can be strained to stagnation when faith has to wait too long.

From around 1877 to 1920, the public and the experts waited for a medical breakthrough. But physical cures for mental illness remained idle dreams, leaving the practical caretakers to concentrate on economical custodial care. Things move so fast these days that I doubt if the lag between molecular biology's promises and payoffs will lead to a parallel stagnant period. However, we know the genetic basis for Huntington's disease, but still have no cure. We need to be sure that training in molecular biology leaves time for residents to learn psychotherapy, and how to care for those who still wait for their scientific salvation.

Around the turn of the last century, scientific medicine came further into the forefront, and psychiatry did get a boost. In 1905, the spirochete *treponema pallidum* was linked to syphilis, and in 1927, Wagner-Jauregg introduced fever therapy for the treatment of patients with syphilitic *dementia paralytica*. These were, of course, momentous breakthroughs with important clinical implications. Clearly, physical treatment was the right thing for dementia caused by syphilis. But belief in the physical roots of insanity did not pay off again until many years later.

At the same time, there was a growing appreciation of scientific psychology. That eventually did some good. At Worcester, the principal players were G. Stanley Hall, who was professor of psychology at nearby Clark University, Hosea Quimby, who was superintendent of the state hospital, and Adolf Meyer, who was one of the great names in American psychiatry. In 1896, Meyer was hired by Quimby and given the title of "Director of Clinics and Pathologist for the Worcester State Hospital." The idea of collaborating with Hall was a major factor in Meyer's going to Worcester. Today, it may be hard to realize how prominent the psychology department at Clark University was during G. Stanley Hall's time. Freud[3] gave his only American lectures at Clark in 1909. His daughter, Anna Freud, spoke there years later, in 1949, although by then her visit was more in memory of her father than a tribute to the Clark psychology department.

Meyer established the hospital as a major center for research and training before his departure for the Pathological Institute of New York City in 1902. In many ways, Meyer was a man whose ideals and methods are still worth emulating. He called his approach to psychiatry "psychobiological" because he believed that mental illnesses resulted from both physical and mental disorders. He put great emphasis on collecting empirical data, and fought for the integration of clinical and research operations within the same walls. He could be called the father of interdisciplinary research in psychiatry, for he tried to involve psychologists, psychiatrists, pathologists, and chemists in the research endeavor. And above all, he was a great educator. The men he trained at Worcester went on to occupy prominent positions in American psychiatry over the next 20 or so years.

Meyer's departure from Worcester in 1902 reflects a recurring theme in academic medicine. Quimby was a visionary state hospital superintendent who wanted to support research. However, Quimby did not understand Meyer's ideas about integrating research and clinical work. The hospital was becoming overcrowded, and getting funds for more personnel was difficult. However, as is too often the case, it was easier to get money for buildings than for people, so in spite of Meyer's objections, Quimby insisted on constructing a small research building outside the hospital walls. The predilection of administrators, legislators, and others for structure over function has been call the Edifice Complex. How much Meyer's leaving for New York in 1902 was a result of Quimby's Edifice Complex and how much it was the promise of a better job, I cannot tell. In any event, he went on to become an international figure in Psychiatry as head of the Henry Phipps Psychiatric Institute at the Johns Hopkins University.

After the departure of Meyer, Worcester State entered another period of decline, although its pioneering work continued in such things as the use of industrial therapy and the restrictions one could place on the application of physical restraints. Quimby's little research building lay fallow until it was borrowed by the Worcester Foundation for Experimental Biology some 30 years later.

Then, in 1920, William Bryan became superintendent. Under him, Worcester had its last renaissance. I arrived 46 years after Meyer left, and enjoyed Worcester at the crest of its last wave. But when that wave broke, Worcester State Hospital had no tomorrow.

52

The Seeds of Deinstitutionalization

I left Worcester in 1950. The Worcester Foundation for Experimental Biology and the Worcester State Hospital continued active collaboration for at least six more years after I left. The years 1955 and 1956 saw the publication of two studies using the hallucinogen LSD-25 (known on the streets as "acid") that had been done by the foundation at the hospital. One study used normal subjects and reported on how LSD-25-induced psychosis affected adrenocortical activity. The other reported that schizophrenic patients were resistant to the psychotogenic effects of LSD-25. I found no joint publications after that date, and the last chapter on the golden age of research at Worcester State Hospital closed definitively in 1968. That was when the Foundation, flush with money from the contraceptive pill, moved to new and elegantly designed buildings in the city of Worcester itself.

Meanwhile, the golden age of psychiatric research was just beginning for academic medicine. By the mid-1950s, almost every medical school in the country was establishing research and residency programs in psychiatry with the help of the National Institute of Mental Health money. Many states and foundations were leaping on the bandwagon with additional support for research on mental illness. At the same time, Worcester was becoming less attractive. After all, what ambitious young physician would go live on a 500-acre farm at the outskirts of Worcester so they could do research on mental illness when gleaming new institutes beckoned with prestigious academic titles? Even more to the point, what spouse would put up with the likes of Worcester State Hospital when more civilized academic surroundings were being offered?

Even before Worcester State Hospital burned down in 1991, it was already dying as a clinical operation. From around 1950 until the old hospital burned, the patient population fell ten-fold, from something near 4,000 to something near 400, and those 400 were housed in a small new building on the grounds of the old hospital. That is an illustration of deinstitutionalization. Perhaps as a function of shifting mentally ill people back to the prisons, from which they had been liberated in 1833, the last occupants of Worcester State Hospital were members of a research team involved with forensic (i.e., prison) psychiatry.

The psychopharmacological revolution's role in deinstitutionalization is easier to explain than is the role of social forces, so that is where we will begin. That revolution was heralded by the discoveries of LSD-25, the hallucinogen, and of chlorpromazine (Thorazine), the first anti-psychotic.

It was in 1938, and well before the pharmacological revolution began, that a chemist at the Swiss drug company Sandoz Inc. was working with a chemical he had named lysergic acid diethylamide. The chemist was A. Hoffman,[4] and since the compound was the twenty-fifth substance in a series of lysergic acid derivatives, he abbreviated its name to LSD-25 for laboratory usage. Hoffman accidentally took an incredibly tiny dose of that chemical and had his famous psychedelic response. However, that chemical did not really have much of an impact on psychiatric thinking until the 1950s. While LSD-25 was not the first hallucinogen ever discovered, it was orders of magnitude more potent than anything else known at that time. This demonstrated that very subtle chemical changes could cause mental illness.

Unfortunately, the hope that LSD-25 would lead us to the cause of schizophrenia, or even provide us with a deeper understanding of the human mind, remains to be fulfilled. The psychosis induced by LSD-25 involves colorful visual hallucinations and sometimes synesthesias (seeing sounds and hearing visions), but auditory hallucinations are rare. LSD-25 paranoia is more like the suspiciousness seen in toxic psychoses, and is rarely organized. By contrast, real schizophrenics are more likely to have auditory hallucinations, and to organize their paranoid delusions. Lastly, some who romanticized schizophrenia in the 1960s and advocated widespread use of LSD-25 claimed that schizophrenics shared the ecstatic feelings of profound insights that LSD-25 users encountered. Sadly, psychedelic-like ecstasy is almost never seen clinically in patients.

Chlorpromazine (Thorazine), the first antipsychotic, was synthesized by the pharmaceutical chemist Paul Charpentier in 1950. Because of its commercial potential, it was studied and exploited a lot faster than was LSD-25. Delay and Deniker's paper on chlorpromazine's anti-psychotic effects appeared in 1952, and within a year the management of psychoses was forever changed. The effect of the drug was nothing short of miraculous. I remember a meeting of the American Psychiatric Association in the 1950s that was as polarized as a Cal-Stanford football game. About half the psychiatrists attending the meeting were hailing chlorpromazine as the ultimate in salvation for schizophrenics, while the other half were condemning it as a chemical straightjacket that did nothing but make psychoanalysis more difficult. As it turned out, both attitudes had some merit.

Soon, the idea of chemical treatments for mental illnesses really caught on. For example, in the 1930s, physicians treating hypertension had tried lithium as a salt substitute, but they gave up on it because of its toxicity. In 1949, John Cade of Australia discovered that lithium was effective as a treatment for bipolar affective disorder, but it was careful clinical studies by Mogens Schou and others during the 1950s that established its clinical use in Europe. The clinical usefulness of lithium was probably greater than that of the anti-psychotic drugs such as chlorpromazine, but its introduction to the United States was a more gradual process than the introduction of chlorpromazine. That was because lithium, being simply an element rather than a synthetic chemical, could not be patented. Because of that, there was no financial incentive for drug companies to get involved and push things along. It was 1970 before the Food and Drug Administration approved lithium for use in the USA. I should add that Smith, Klein, and French, the drug company that sold chlorpromazine, deserves credit for helping out with the clinical trials of lithium.

The story of lithium is also an answer to some physicians who call themselves "Orthomolecular," and generally are opposed to double blind testing of their remedies because they already know they work. They often use natural, un-patentable substances, and claim that members of the psychiatric "establishment" do not adopt their treatments because they are dupes of the drug industry, which opposes their remedies because no profit can be made from them. But in fact, on the basis of the double-blind trials of lithium in Europe, the psychiatric establishment in the United States labored hard to get lithium approved for manic-depressive illness in this country.

The enthusiasm for designing chemicals to treat mental illness continued and produced the tricyclic antidepressants in the early 1960s. These had been designed to compete with phenothiazines as anti-schizophrenia drugs. But while ineffective in schizophrenia, they turned out to work on depression. The first drugs of that class were amitriptyline (Elavil) and imipramine (Tofranil). They were, however, not quite as revolutionary in the treatment of depression as were lithium in the treatment of bipolar disorder and phenothiazines in the treatment of schizophrenia. Indeed, there are some psychiatrists today who still argue that electroconvulsive therapy remains the most effective treatment for depression. Still, because of the unfair, adverse press given electroconvulsive treatment, the tricyclics meant that many more depressives would get help.

To round things out, the so-called minor tranquilizers made their appearance about the same time, with meprobamate (Miltown) being synthesized in 1950, and chlordiazepoxide (Librium), the first of the benzodiazepines, becoming available in the United States around 1960. The minor tranquilizers did not bring many long term benefits to patients with major mental illnesses, but they made a significant difference in treating anxiety and managing acute episodes of agitation, for they were incomparably safer than were the barbiturates (e.g., Amytal). Barbiturate overdoses killed by stopping breathing, and the margin for error was uncomfortably small. On the other hand, unless someone adds alcohol, about the only way to kill a patient with benzodiazepines is to give so many pills that the patient chokes on them.

Since then, drug development has continued apace. There are whole new classes of antidepressants. There are new drugs for narcolepsy, new drugs for attention deficit disorder, new mood stabilizers, new atypical antipsychotics, etc. But these latest drugs did not have much to do with deinstitutionalization, so I will not discuss them here.

I have given a hasty overview of the whole psychopharmacological revolution, but it was the antipsychotic drugs and lithium that, during the 50s and 60s, helped most in emptying mental hospitals. Patients with acute psychotic episodes could be spared some of the suffering and humiliation that resulted from their illnesses. When the psychosis remitted in such people, it was less difficult for them to resume a normal life. Some chronic patients who had been disruptive or even dangerous could now be cared for at home or in halfway houses. Some of the patients in the mental hospitals who were treated with the new drugs even returned to work. Deinstitutionalization was a positive thing for many people.

However, the early anti-psychotic drugs were better for "positive symptoms," such as hallucinations and delusions, than for negative symptoms, such as autism and withdrawal. The sight of drugged schizophrenic patients sitting passively in day care facilities led some to damn the antipsychotic drugs as chemical straitjackets. It is only in the last 10 years that the so-called atypical antipsychotics such as clozapine (Clozaril) have come on the scene, and they appear to offer relief from both the positive and negative symptoms of schizophrenia.

I would be the last person to undervalue the impact of psychopharmacology on the field of mental health. Nevertheless, it was the social and political forces, albeit reinforced by the advances in psychopharmacology, which became the prime movers of change in the 1960s and 1970s. Indeed, the cart of deinstitutionalization had already started to move before the horse of psychopharmacology appeared on the scene.

Around 1950 and just after I left Worcester State Hospital, Flower, the superintendent, and Rothschild, the clinical director, began to organize psychiatrists, psychologists, and social workers into discharge teams. These were sent to scour the hospital for patients who could be returned to the community. Yes, there were pressures coming from the state legislature based on economic motives, but these were nothing new. The major driving force in the "return-to-the-community" movement of the 1950s was a more general philosophical one, just as the original establishment of the hospital for "moral therapy" in the 1830s reflected society-wide philosophical trends.

We were headed for the 1960s when civil rights, protection of workers, prison reform, acceptance of alternative lifestyles, and support for medical research were all on the upswing. It was clear that patients tended to become institutionalized and to settle in more or less comfortably as permanent wards of the state. This was aided and abetted by families and communities that were happy to be rid of members who were at times disruptive and were at best marginally productive. While relatively rare in the United States, there were examples of both institutionalization and electroconvulsive treatment being used as techniques of control and oppression rather than as aids in therapy. But involuntary treatments and the warehousing of deviants went against the grain of the liberal *zeitgeist* of the 1960s.

Borne on the waves of this revolutionary approach to social justice, many wanted to discard all the old treatments for the mentally ill wholesale, and carve out wholly new approaches. For example, a small Dutch village supported itself economically by taking in mentally ill patients for pay, and caring for them by placing them in the homes of the villagers. That would seem obviously to be more humane than large state hospitals. That village became rather irrationally idealized, while the social, economic, and cultural differences between the Netherlands and the United States were conveniently ignored.

Nevertheless, a noble sense of mission fired the advocates for this new field of "community psychiatry." As crusaders, they set out to close the state hospitals and stop the use of electroconvulsive therapy. Patients who had been deprived of their civil liberties and relegated to dehumanizing warehouses would be restored to their rightful place in society. Meanwhile, psychotic behavior was being hailed by some members of the Age of Aquarius as evidence of enlightenment, or at worst as merely deviant behavior. After all, that culture supported the use of drugs to induce hallucinations, and schizophrenics were considered gifted because they were able to hallucinate all on their own.

In the 1960s, I was teaching in San Francisco at Langley Porter Institute, which at the time was part UCSF and part state hospital. It was also only a few blocks from the famous Haight-Ashbury district of San Francisco. Young, middle-class, middle-Western children with stars in their eyes and flowers in their hair drifted into communes. There they sometimes emulated recently deinstitutionalized schizophrenics. Psychotics were often members of communes, where their delusions were tolerated and even encouraged. Then, with the right combination of odd social norms, sleep deprivation, and assorted chemicals, some "flower children" developed what we called hysterical schizophrenia. They came to emergency rooms with odd deliria, and so were given high doses of phenothiazines.

When the side effects of the "therapeutic" drugs from the emergency room began, these otherwise healthy "flower children" were convinced that they really were crazy, and so were admitted to Langley Porter. We found that recovery from antipsychotic drug overdose, reassurance, and a call home to mother produced complete and lasting remissions.

During the same era, when I tried to teach medical students about schizophrenia, I was attacked as a dupe of the oppressive establishment, and was informed that mental illness was nothing but a myth used by the State to enforce conformity! I am still amazed when I recall that era. Intelligent 22 year olds were so full of themselves and their generation's ideologies that they would refuse to consider empirical data, and could discount a senior professor as an idiot out of hand. Fortunately, that craze only lasted a couple of years, or I would have given up teaching.

Coincidentally, well-trained and well-meaning mental health workers (myself among them, for a while) were setting up houses where psychotic patients could experience their psychoses in supportive environments, and so convert their episodes of madness from mental illnesses into journeys toward greater personal growth. One such group that I was associated with called itself Diabasis House (*diabasis* from the Greek for "passing through"). As in the old state hospital, occasional patients remitted with minimal scarring. However, tragically, we learned that when manic patients go off their lithium to "experience and work through their psychosis," many become unresponsive to lithium when their voyages of self-discovery land them in hell and their physicians try to restart their treatment.

I remember a beautiful lady I will call Brenda. Her mild hypo-mania while on lithium had made her exceptionally popular among the rich and socially prominent. Then she met a psychologist, who thought re-experiencing childhood trauma would cure everything. He induced her to stop lithium and start sandbox play therapy. I inherited Brenda in a florid psychosis after she had physically demolished a fancy dinner party and alienated all but one of her socialite acquaintances. Lithium no longer had any effect on Brenda, and I was reduced to using carbamazepine (Tegretol). In her case, the dose that controlled her mania and the dose that left her embarrassingly intoxicated were painfully close. Brenda and I struggled together for about a year, making tiny changes in medication and trying to re-establish some semblance of her lost social life. Finally, Brenda left San Francisco to stay with her parents in another state, and I breathed a sigh of relief.

To me, psychiatry has always been primarily a study of individuals. Surprisingly, in the literature of the community mental health movement, references to particular human beings tend to be absent. Instead, community mental health writers seem concerned exclusively with catchment areas, day care centers, residential facilities, follow-up programs, and other bureaucratic entities that need administration. I wonder if psychiatrists, who had been dismayed by the difficulty of treating psychotic patients, found that committee meetings, political activism, and an abstract involvement with the mentally ill offered a welcomed change.

Dan Weisburd[5] wrote an introduction to a special issue of *The Journal of the California Alliance for the Mentally Ill* (CAMI) that reported on the development of patient-friendly Integrated Service Agencies. In that introduction, he described his attempts to get treatment for his schizophrenic son. Recounting his dissatisfaction with the mental health systems available at the time, he wrote:

> I have this gut feeling it should all be focused on the ill person, on *his* needs. But, instead *programs* are funded *and people are put on waiting lists.*

I cannot forget Frieda Fromm-Reichman saying, ''One at a time was enough for God. So it should be for me.'' It still seems to me that ''compassion for a diagnostic group'' and ''empathy for populations'' are oxymoronic.

53

The Unholy Alliance

When right-wing, "fiscal accountability" politicians formed an unholy alliance with left-wing, "free the people" idealists, that alliance produced what has been called "the anti-psychiatry movement." I have already mentioned *Madness in the Streets* by R.J. Isaac and V.C. Armat. This book was published in 1990, but is out of print now. While it is available in libraries, I have attached its table of contents as an appendix to provide a clear outline of the steps that led us to our current bizarre mental health system. Although the book is a polemic, it gives an accurate picture of the anti-psychiatry movement. It documents, blow by blow, how left-wing libertarians (who denied the existence of mental illness) made common cause with right-wing Republicans (who wanted to save money), and how together they gutted mental health services. Both groups operated from grand principles, and neither had any interest in seeing whether their theories worked in the real world. Both had such faith in their rather incompatible beliefs that they were never tempted to follow up on the results of their decisions. In effect, by denying the existence of mental illness, they dismantled care for seriously disordered individuals, and turned them out on the streets, back to their families, or into criminals.

Six years after *Madness in the Streets*, Fuller Torrey's[6] *Out of the Shadows: Confronting America's Mental Illness Crisis* was published. It details the consequences of deinstitutionalization, and is another fine polemic. With meticulously researched statistics and dismaying case histories, Torry comes down in favor of involuntary treatment for some cases of mental illness. I wish I could be as sure as he is, but there are some thorny issues hidden in the easy solutions.

In spite of my misgivings about polemics in general, I was moved by both of the books mentioned above. In contrast, there are the distorted ravings and cult-like tactics of the Scientologists and their captive psychiatrist, Dr. Peter Breggin. They have appalled me, and their motivations still elude me. I have heard various explanations: for example, that they are driven by greed, by hunger for power, or by lust for revenge against psychiatry in general, because their founder, L. Ron Hubbard, had bad experiences with psychiatrists during some of his psychotic episodes. What I do know is that they are the entirely degenerate remains of the basically well-meaning anti-psychiatry movement started by genuine libertarian idealists, but now degraded into purely destructive nonsense.

I am sympathetic to Torrey's suggestions for changes in the mental health system, although I think we have to take a cautious approach in recommending that people be given drugs and other treatments that they do not want. Fortunately, the search for solutions to the issues of involuntary medication and mandatory outpatient treatment goes on in other states and other countries.

In New York State, there have been heated arguments and litigation concerning what is known as Kendra's Law. This law involves a complex scheme whereby psychotic patients in remission can give permission for involuntary medication during their psychotic episodes. However, a correspondent of mine in New York told me recently that Kendra's Law had accomplished little except to offer some comfort to the parents of Kendra Webdale, who was pushed in front of the "N" train in New York by a schizophrenic.

I present the following true story as a concrete illustration of the problem. The headline of an article published in the Marin County Independent Journal (published in Novato, California) on November 10, 2000 reads: "Woman charged with rare hate crime." According to the paper, the victim was going to get his boat when the woman, "shouting obscenities and accusing the man of raping her, poked him in the stomach with a six foot oar and then clubbed him six times with it." The woman was well-known locally as "The Man Hater," and was on probation for a similar assault on a United Parcel Service man. She was charged with assault with a deadly weapon and hate crime enhancement. Hate crimes usually involve race or sexual preference (e.g., homosexuality), but rarely gender. Nevertheless, the "Man Hater" could face up to seven years in prison. No mention is made of mental illness, and the obvious diagnosis is left as an exercise for the reader. I would give her a 90 percent chance of being freed from her terrors and returned to a more rewarding life if medicated. The chance of her accepting medication voluntarily, I would fear, is zero. The probability of prison helping the "Man Hater" is also zero.

In California, a convicted felon has lost only those rights that would interfere with control and incarceration. In other words, an imprisoned criminal has all the rights and privileges that you and I have, except those that could help him to escape. There is an elaborate procedure for the involuntary administration of psychoactive medications in prison that parallels the civil procedures. It is known as the Keyhea Procedure, after a 1977 court decision. In brief, emergency medication can be given when the person is "an immediate danger to self or to others or is unable to care for self." There is a 72-hour emergency period, but first the patient must be videotaped. Then, there must be a local hearing in 10 days, and a court hearing before an administrative judge within 21 days. In prison, medication can be continued for a new inmate only if there have been serious threats to self or others since arrest. By contrast, in new cases, continued treatment is allowed if there have been threats since the last medication hearing. But now imagine that you are a correctional officer running a prison, and your medical officer requests a procedure that involves videotaping, two legal hearings, and an unimaginable mountain of associated paper work. I am sure you can appreciate why all of this is a great incentive to leave a noncompliant patient unmedicated if at all possible.

An interesting law in Wisconsin has survived a challenge in the Wisconsin Supreme Court.[7] The law allows involuntary treatment of mentally ill individuals who "are clearly dangerous to themselves because their incapacity to make informed medication or treatment decisions makes them more vulnerable to severely harmful deterioration than those who are competent to make such decisions." (I hope that wretched run-on sentence does not reflect the abilities of our Wisconsin allies.)

In the movie *A Beautiful Mind*, which was based on Silvia Nassar's biography of Nobel Laureate John Nash, the actor portraying Nash during his schizophrenic episodes was magnificent, and deserved the Oscar he won. However, the movie left out the fact that, according to the book, Nash's son is also schizophrenic, untreated, and a continuing, almost unsupportable, burden on Nash and his wife. I suppose it is enough that the movie makers gave a wide audience some feeling for the problem of schizophrenia, even if they topped it off with a less than candid happy ending. Perhaps it would indeed have been too much to burden the public with the story of the Nash's apparently intractable problems with a medication-non-compliant paranoid schizophrenic son.

The tragedy of the untreated and untreatable schizophrenic child is so common that I feel uncertain about elaborating on it, because the odds are that you have some awful examples among your own friends, or even worse, in your own family. Often it is the favorite child who turns into an incomprehensible monster. The schizophrenic is almost always frustratingly unresponsive to reason, sometimes physically threatening, and occasionally dangerous. Even away from home, he or she may be financially draining, and often presents the family with one emotionally exhausting crisis after another. Examples include unwanted pregnancies and transcontinental attempts to pick up the pieces after near-fatal street drug overdoses.

But there is hope. The older drugs did relieve the primary symptoms, but made most patients miserable. While some patients with terrifying delusions welcomed relief at any cost, many patients naturally prefer delusions of grandeur to a dulled mind and stiffened muscles. But a host of new antipsychotics now make it much easier to get compliance. Examples of the new drugs include Abilify (aripirizole), Clozaril (clozapine), Geodon (ziprasidone), Resperdol (respiridone), Seroquil (quietapine), and Zyprexia (olanzapine). A colleague who works in an emergency room remarked recently about an experience with one of those new drugs. He said that, for the first time in his experience, he had given an antipsychotic injection to wildly excited patient, and then had the patient later say, "Gee Doc, thanks for that shot!"

There are also community mental health services where workers, some of whom may be former patients, offer intensive client-oriented care. By becoming closely involved with their clients—for example, becoming payees for the clients' welfare checks, etc.—they get regular attendance. With close, sensitive, personal relationships, and by furnishing a number of small services, such as accompanied shopping trips, they bring about remarkable changes. They even manage to get surprising compliance with medication regimes. One program that I had contact with gathered data on clients before and after the program started. For the same clients and for an equivalent period of time, before the program, there were 1,785 hospital visits and 797 days in jail. When the program was operating, there were 640 hospital visits and 256 days in jail. Obviously, over and above humanitarian concerns, good care saves money.

One of the most daunting problems is that of substance abuse by the seriously mentally ill. While some patients refuse all drugs, others will take any drugs you offer. Unfortunately, patients in the latter group take their prescription drugs in unpredictable ways, then add alcohol, marijuana, cocaine, methamphetamine, heroin, and what have you. The result is a psychopharmacologist's nightmare.

So what are the solutions to the problems of involuntary medication and voluntary substance abuse? The desiderata come down to the old "greatest good for the greatest number." We want laws that will (a) guard society against violence, (b) protect the incompetent from self-harm, and (c) safeguard civil liberty.

With respect to the privilege of refusing treatment, including medication, hundreds of different programs to address that problem are being used in various states and around the world. I have inquired informally about a few of these "experiments in nature." Some are interesting, but there are others I do not want to see repeated in my state. But I do not see why the National Institute of Mental Health cannot at least collate the results of these experiments and score them according to the three criteria listed above.

With respect to mental patients' use of illicit drugs, although it is not a privilege that comes with citizenship, ordinary jails have not been effective in controlling substance abuse either outside or inside. My attempts to learn about the long-term results of forensic hospitalization have not been successful. I have seen remarkable results from diversionary outpatient programs, where patients choose to attend special group and individual therapy sessions as a condition for parole and an alternative to jail. I have also heard counselors who work in some of these successful outpatient programs remark that, no matter how wonderfully patients respond to involuntary inpatient treatment, if patients feel that treatments have been shoved down their throats, they will relapse on discharge. For patients to continue with their medication and to remain "clean and sober," they must acknowledge their illness and accept responsibility for their actions. Not surprisingly, successful substance abuse programs, such as Alcoholics Anonymous, require just such acknowledgement of illness and acceptance of personal responsibility. Peer groups of patients with major psychoses are harder to manage than are groups of alcoholics, but the idea, at least, is worth a try.

The old asylums cared for the seriously mentally ill, so I have put the most emphasis on schizophrenia and bipolar affective disorders, the so-called major mental illnesses. But the depressions and their fellow travelers, the anxiety disorders and obsessive-compulsive disorders, are about 10 times more common. These are not really minor mental illnesses, for their physical and economic costs are well documented. Treatments for these illnesses now, in most cases, are nearly "no-brainers." Sadly, getting general physicians and the public to recognize depression has proven to be daunting.

So there you have my views on the ups and downs of psychiatry, with the Worcester State Hospital as a metaphor. In the 1980s, the community mental health movement flourished, psychopharmacology continued to explode, and most of the old asylums wasted away. A small mental health center had been built on the grounds of Worcester State Hospital to house the residual patients. But the grim old Victorian castle I had known and loved, referred to in the press of the time as the "Bell Tower Building," was dying.

One day in the spring of 1991, the old building burned. Children in a special education program were having an outing on the grounds in back of the hospital when the fire broke out, and their evacuation delayed the firemen enough to let the blaze get totally out of hand. A news reporter on the spot at the time commented that fortunately the children were not frightened, and seemed to enjoy the spectacle. It seems ironic that such a venerable center of treatment and research should perish at a time when research money was so available. In the South, they used to

The End. Front page of the *Worcester Telegram and Gazette*, July 22, 1991, showing the old hospital burning down. **Courtesy of the Worcester Telegram & Gazette.**

speak of "the lousy calf that lived through the winter and died in the spring."

The old Worcester State Hospital is gone forever. The research done there is archived in libraries and indices, but those of us who experienced Worcester State at its high point can not anticipate such immortality. Hence these memoirs.

54

Postscript: So What? With Notes on the Culture of Caring

Millions of people are enjoying the advances that psychiatry has made in this last half century. Yet many of those who need help most are no better off, or are in even worse condition than the patients I knew at Worcester. Why should you care?

Consider if you will that each of us has a central nervous system that contains a model of our self, a model of the so-called real world, and real time simulations of the interactions between those models. Most of this goes on via chemical reactions in the jelly-like things we call our brains. We have barely begun to understand the brain and its chemistry, and like Alice remarked in *Wonderland*, at each step things become "curiouser and curiouser." Someone commented that if our brains were simple enough to understand, we would be too simple to understand them. That is a clever remark, but I am not sure I would count the neuroscientists out yet, for they are making dazzling advances at an accelerating rate. Nonetheless, the complexity that we can see so far does indeed boggle the mind.

At any time, about 90 percent of us have brains that have come to more or less the same conclusions. To me, that fact seems as improbable as breaking the bank at Monte Carlo. If, for the nonce, you and I are among the 90 percent who seem to agree in general on what reality is, does that suggest that we should be less caring for the 10 percent whose models seem at variance with ours and who see or hear things that the rest of us do not? Then, humanitarian concerns aside, mental illness can have devastating effects on the families of the mentally ill, as I have already described.

Today we work under "managed care," controlled by the executive-burdened for-profit insurance industry. Such mindless bureaucracies are the antithesis of the culture of caring. I remember Louis Hill, Chief of Psychotherapy at the Shepherd and Enoch Pratt Hospital in Towson, Maryland, saying that a running resident physician was not a thinking resident physician. What second-party payer is going to find profit in telling doctors to slow down and think?

While the extravagant hopes we had for psychoanalysis in the 1940s are no longer tenable, there is ample evidence that certain types of psychotherapy are cost effective. In some cases, combining drugs and psychotherapy is even more effective, and in the long run less costly, than either alone. Evidence for the superiority of combined pharmacotherapy and psychotherapy is most compelling in cases of depression. But in any medical situation, a trusting relationship with a supportive physician can be critical. It helps the patient to weather those almost inevitable peculiar feelings and other minor adverse events at the start of drug therapy, and to remain compliant so that maximum benefits can be obtained. The most wonderful drug will not help the patient who refuses to take it.

In the case of some antidepressants, stopping medication results in such prompt physical discomfort that future compliance is almost guaranteed. But the manic-depressive can, without immediate consequences, go off of lithium until the next attack, and if that next episode is one of mania, the ensuing grandiosity is likely to block compliance with any medical advice.

Psychiatric residents still need the time to learn psychotherapy, or at least to learn the skills of listening and interviewing. Even compassion can be taught, or at least enhanced by teaching. I think it would also be useful if they had time to take part in clinical research. None of this is likely if teaching clinics are expected to pay their ways. I also think psychologists and psychotherapists should be given required courses in the elements of psychopharmacology. At the rate neuropsychopharmacology is leaping ahead, psychologists and counselors should not have to become independent physicians, but should know enough basic pharmacokinetics (how the drug moves to and from its site of action) and pharmacodynamics (what the drug does at its site of action) to collaborate intelligently with a pharmacotherapist.

Today there are residency programs turning out gifted psychotherapists and productive clinical researchers. There are non-medical psychotherapists who are surprisingly sophisticated about pharmacology. There are police who are trained to recognize mental illness and to deal with it humanely. There are community programs that have been highly successful at keeping patients on their medications and getting them back to work. One effective program is based on fostering patient responsibility, with counselors playing roles of specialists and advisors rather than acting as authoritarian directors. Obviously, since the things I would suggest already exist, they are neither revolutionary nor beyond reasonable expectations.

Our impatient society is one of the biggest obstacles to effective care of the mentally ill. Video games and movies offer plots with fast and often violent resolutions. Road rage erupts when drivers are delayed for trivial lengths of time. Politicians live from one poll to the next. Voters demand quick answers, more prisons, and harsher punishment. Activists find that outrageous promises and outright dishonesty give them the best chance of getting what they want from legislators, and their extreme claims attract the press and so provide a bonus of narcissistic gratification.

Politicians' needs for quick results impact the care of the mentally ill. For example, Dr. Jim Satterfield was one of the pioneers in the treatment of childhood attention deficit-hyperactivity disorder. Some years back, he approached a sympathetic politician with hard data showing a dramatic reduction in prison time of inner city teenagers with attention deficit disorder when a program of combined pharmacotherapy and socialization training had been instituted at age seven or eight.[8]

Jim reasoned that kids learn social skills from other kids, but hyperactive kids are a pain in the ass to their peers as well as to their parents and teachers, and so they end up under-socialized. In other words, without drugs, they could not get along with their peers enough to practice social skills, even if a psychologist tried to teach them such skills. With drugs alone they still did not have the elementary social skills to get along with their peers where the social skills could be further practiced and developed. But by both training them in the social skills needed for getting along and giving them drugs for a few years, they did very well.

Over and above any benefits to the kids, it was clear that the savings in taxpayers' dollars would be impressive. Sadly, that sympathetic politician told Jim that he could not afford to put his job on the line for a benefit that would come long after he had retired from public office.

The National Institute of Mental Health sponsored a study that ostensibly measured the effects of drugs and psychotherapy on treatment of attention deficit-hyperactivity disorder. Rather than trying to replicate Jim Satterfield's work, they tried their own brief psychotherapy and found it did not add much to the benefits from the drugs. The hubris that seems natural, and perhaps essential, in researchers makes them reluctant to repeat a study exactly the way some one else did it.

Even if it were not for that, the number of unknown but potentially relevant variables in clinical research is daunting. Physical experiments can be controlled more or less with precision, but in psychiatry, social changes can alter all the rules of the game. Remember that "Moral Therapy" was a great success at Worcester in the early part of the nineteenth century. It stopped working around the middle of that century, presumably because of change from an almost pure WASP population to a more heterogeneous one. Unfortunately, however difficult it may be, we must constantly try to test and re-test our assumptions.

Recently, a colleague told me that he saw evidence of an over-correction, headed towards easier civil commitments and involuntary treatment without proper supervision. Can we look forward to another unreasoned cycle in the care for the mentally ill? Torrey's *Out of the Shadows* is no less a polemic than is Sasz's *The Myth of Mental Illness.*[9] The latter book argues for the early position of anti-psychiatry. While I personally have little respect for the arguments of Dr. Sasz, and generally agree with Torrey, polemics are polemics, and are not evenhanded attempts to cover the pros and cons of complex issues.

For the long run, I believe our best intellectual tools are reductionism and empiricism. Reductionism means that when we face a new problem, we may have to break it into smaller pieces before we can begin solving it. Sweeping universal solutions that we looked for in the 1940s are almost inevitably bad. By empiricism, I mean that any theory should be tested against reality. First, the theory must in principle be testable. For example, if someone says, "When no one is diagnosed as mentally ill, then mental illness will cease to exist," you should answer, "Interesting, but how would you know if that were not so? That is to say, how would you test your theory?" Put another way, we must try to simplify and limit the questions that we ask nature so that she can give us intelligible answers. Beware of grand principles that seem to explain everything but that cannot be tested. Enjoy them as poetry or use them as heuristics, but do not trust them. The most gifted and productive minds have arrived at the above principals, yet it takes no great intellect to appreciate them.

You have my memories and my opinions. If you have believed me uncritically, then I have failed. The hope for the mentally ill lies in public awareness, in a healthy skepticism, and in testing our ideas so we can know when we are wrong. All of that must, of course, be leavened with that combination of respect and empathy called compassion. I have lived long, worked hard, and loved my work. I am grateful that I have seen, and even participated in, so much of the history of psychiatry. I have seen evolution and revolution in the treatment of mental illness. I have watched the ebb and flow of human compassion in those administering such treatment. I have known the mentally ill as teacher, therapist, and friend. I hope you will agree with me that how society treats its most vulnerable members tells us who we really are.

****

In the years since I finished this book, both the cost and the absurdity of handling the severely mentally ill with the criminal justice system has become widely recognized, and among the potential solutions, two (that have already been mentioned) seem clearly the most promising. One is based on developing laws that force patients to take their medicine. Illustrative "outpatient commitment" approaches are reflected in Kendra's Law (mentioned earlier), and that approach has its own non-profit foundation, The Treatment Advocacy Center, (www.psychlaws.org).

They have evidence that their approach works in a wide range of cases, and I personally have seen something like it work in a situation where a euthymic (neither manic nor depressed) bipolar patient agreed to involuntary medication at the first signs of another manic episode.

The other approach seems diametrically opposite. Using staff that usually includes ex-patients, the "clients" are asked to set up goals and to examine how their various actions affect their chances of reaching one or more of their goals. The "case managers" can help the client examine the consequences of an action and suggest alternatives. They can inform the client about resources. But they never tell the client what to do. Goals imply hope, and consequences imply responsibility. Taking medication is the patient's responsibility. Clinics based on this "Recovery Centered Clinical System" are being set up by the Telecare Corp. (www.telecare. com), a for-profit business. They have impressive data on reducing arrests and emergency room visits in a group of chronically mentally ill patients. They also lean heavily on the writings of Patricia Deegan.[10]

That leaves us with several delightfully answerable questions. Do the programs differ in the type of patient that they help the most? How do their long term results compare? How much money per patient does each system cost? I hope the future brings answers that are data-driven rather than faith- or theory-based.

Appendix

Contents of *Madness in the Streets,* referred to in Chapter 50, by Isaac, R. J. and Armat, V. C., (New York: MacMillan, New York, N.Y.

Introduction: The Shame of the Streets

PART I. Anti-Psychiatry: Birth of a Social Delusion

I. The Origins of Anti-Psychiatry

2. Mental Illness as Label: The Academy Joins Anti-Psychiatry

PART II. The Vision of Community Care

3. Community Mental Health Centers: The Dream

4. Community Mental Health Centers: The Reality

PART III. The Law Becomes Deranged

5. The Rise of the Mental Health Bar

6. Hospitalization Under Attack: The Major Legal Cases

7. From the Right to Treatment to the Right to Refuse Treatment

PART IV. The War Against Treatment

8. The Rise of the Ex-Patient Movement

9. Psychosurgery: The First Domino

10. Electroconvulsive Therapy: The Second Domino

11. Psychoactive Drugs: The Last Domino

PART V. Families as Mental Institutions

12. The Right to Be Crazy

13. The Specter of Violence

PART VI. The Mentally Ill in the Community

14. Winging It with Pilot Programs in the Community

15. Community Services Are Not Enough

Conclusion: Forging a New Bipartisan Consensus

Notes

Index

This Table of Contents was copied with the generous permission of The Treatment Advocacy Center.

Notes

ACKNOWLEDGMENTS

1. Derivery, C. & Bernadet, P. (2003). *Enfermez-les Tout!* Laffont, Paris, France.
2. Deikman, A.J. (2003). *Them and Us.* Bay Tree Publishing, Berkeley, CA.
3. Goldman, W., McCulloch, J., Cuffel, B., Zarin, D.A., Suarez, A., & Burns, B.J. (1998). Outpatient utilization patterns of integrated and split psychotherapy and pharmacotherapy for depression. *Psychiatric Services.* 49: 477–482
4. Grob, G.N. (1966). *The State and the Mentally Ill. A history of Worcester State Hospital in Massachusetts, 1830–1920* University of North Carolina Press, Chapel Hill, NC.
5. Jamison, K.R. (1995). *The Unquiet Mind.* A.A. Knopf, New York, NY.
6. Linehan, M.M. (1993). *Cognitive-Behavioral Treatment of Borderline Personality Disorders.* Guilford Press, New York, NY.
7. Strunk, W & White, E.B. (2000). *The Elements of Style. Fourth Edition.* Pearson, Allyn and Bacon, New York, NY.

INTRODUCTION

1. Morisey, P.J. (1980). *The Enduring Asylum. Cycles of institutional reforms at Worcester State Hospital.* Grune & Stratton, Inc., New York, NY.

PART I

1. Nasar, S. (1998). *A Beautiful Mind.* Simon and Schuster, New York, NY.
2. Kesey, K. (1962). *One Flew Over the Cuckoo's Nest* Viking Press, New York, NY.
3. American Psychiatric Association. (1994). *Diagnostic and Statistical Manual of Mental Disorders. Fourth Edition,*American Psychiatric Association, Washington, D.C.

4. Shem, S. (1978). *House of God*. R. Marek, New York, N Y.

5. Wiener, N. (1950). *The Human Use of Human Beings; Cybernetics and Society*. Houghton Mifflin, Boston, MA.

PART 2

1. Green, H. (pseudonym for Joanne Greenberg). (1964). *I Never Promised You a Rose Garden*. Holt, Rineheart and Winston, New York, NY.

2. Kanas, N. (1996). *Group Therapy of Schizophrenic Patients*. American Psychiatric Press, Washington, D.C.

3. James, W. (1890). *The Principles of Psychology*. Henry Holt, New York, NY.

PART 3

1. Zilboorg, G. (1941). *A History of Medical Psychology*. W.W. Norton, New York, NY.

2. Bookhammer, R.S. et al. (1966). A five-year clinical follow-up study of schizophrenicstreated by Rosen's "direct analysis" compared withcontrols. *American Journal of Psychiatry*. 123: 602–604.

3. Deutsch, H. (1973). *The Psychology of Women. A Psychoanalytic Interpretation*. Bantam Books. New York, NY.

4. Shakow, D. (1977). The Worcester State Hospital research on schizophrenia (1927–1964). *Psychological Issues,* 10:208–315

5. Hoagland, H. (1974). *The Road to Yesterday*. Privately Printed. Worcester, MA.

6. Berg, P. & Singer, M. (1998). Inspired Choices. *Science*. 282: 873–874.

7. Parkinson, C.N. (1957). *Parkinson's Law, and Other Studies in Administration*. 47:1940–1951. Houghton Mifflin, Boston, Ma.

8. Davis, W. (1985). *The Serpent and the Rainbow*. Simon & Schuster, New York, NY.

9. Wortis, J. (1995). *Fragments of an Analysis with Freud.*Reprinted as*Analysis with Freud. (Masterworks Series)* Jason Aranson, New York, N. Y.

10. Wortis, J. (1996). *Psychiatric Tidbits*. Society of Biological Psychiatry.

11. Lettvin, J.Y., Maturana, H.R., McCulloch, W.S. & Pitts, W.H. (1965). What the frog's eye tells the frog's brain. *Proceedings of the Institute of Radio Engineers.*47: 1940–1951.

12. Freud, S. (1927). *The Future of an Illusion*. in J. Strachey, ed. and trans. (1962). *The Standard Edition of the Complete Psychological Works of Sigmund Freud. Vol. 21*, Hogarth Press and Inst. of Psychoanalysis, London.

13. Beck, A.T., Emery, G. & Greenberg, R.L. (1985). *Anxiety Disorders and Phobias; a Cognitive perspective*. Basic Books, New York, NY.

14. Weissman, M.M., Markowitz, J.C., & Klerman, G.L. (2000). *The Comprehensive Guide to Interpersonal Psychotherapy*. Basic Books, New York, NY.

15. Shapiro, F. (2001). *Eye Movement Desensitization and Reprocessing*. Guilford Press, New York, NY.

16. Bush, N., Gassner, S. (1988). A description and clinical research application of control-mastery theory. *Clinical Social Work Journal,* 16:231–242.

17. Edmonds, D. & Edinow, J. (2001). *Wittgenstein's Poker.* HarperCollins Publishers Inc., New York NY.

18. Popper K. (1945). *The Open Society and Its Enemies.* Routledge and Kegan Paul, London.

PART 4

1. Freud, S. (1885). *Projects for a Scientific Psychology.* in J. Strachey, ed. and trans. (1962). *The Standard Edition of the Complete Psychological Works of Sigmund Freud. Vol. 3.* Hogarth Press and Inst. of Psychoanalysis, London.

2. Isaac, R.J. & Armat, V.C. (1990). *Madness in the Streets.* MacMillan, New York, NY.

3. Freud, S. (1933). *New Introductory Lectures in Psychoanalysis.* Hogarth, London.

4. Hoffmann, A. (1979). *LSD, My Problem Child,* cited in Shulgin, A. & Shulgin, A..(1997). *THIKAL.*(pp 493.). Transform Press, Berkeley, CA.

5. Weisburd, D. (1993). Publisher's Note. *The Journal of the California Alliance for the Mentally Ill.* 4; 1

6. Torrey, E.F. (1996). *Out of the Shadows.*John Wiley, New York, N.Y.

7. Binder, E. (2002). Wisconsin court rejects attempt to narrow commitment law.*Psychiatric News.* 27: 13.

8. Satterfield, J.H., Satterfield B.T., & Schell A.M. (1987).Therapeutic interventions to prevent delinquency in hyperactive boys.*Journal of American Academy of Child and Adolescent Psychiatry.* 26:56–64

9. Szasz, T. (1962). *The Myth of Mental Illness : foundations of a theory of personal conduct.*Hoeber-Harper, New York, N.Y.

10. Degan. P. (1990). Spirit breaking: When the helping professions hurt. *The Humanistic Psychologist,* 18:301–313.

Index

A Beautiful Mind, 24, 36, 179
Antidepressant, 28, 151, 172, 184
Antipsychotic(s), 5, 8, 16, 23, 39, 82, 112–113, 171–175, 180

Barbiturates, 5–6, 39, 44–46, 51, 55, 76, 173
Behavior Therapy, 151
Bleuler, Manfried, 39, 139
Brazier, M. A. B. (Molly), 61–64
Bromism, 50–52

Catatonic (catatonia), 18, 38–39, 49, 75, 94–96, 119, 122, 146
Chloral Hydrate, 54
Chlorpromazine, 5, 22, 185, 171–172
Clozaril, 82, 173, 180
Cognitive Behavior Therapy, 127, 151
Compulsion (compulsive), 31, 43,164, 181
Control-Mastery Theory, 153

Dementia, 7–9, 36, 51, 56, 73, 75, 89, 104–105, 167
Depression (depressive), 7, 28–30, 39, 51, 75, 84, 95, 114–117, 122–123, 127–128, 139–140, 148, 151, 164, 172, 181, 187
Deutsch, Felix, 125–128
Diazepam, 8, 55

ECT (electroconvulsive or electroshock therapy), 5, 24, 28–30, 74, 114, 116, 146–147, 172, 174, 190
EEG (electroencephalogram), 17, 19–20, 22, 28, 34, 42, 61–64, 101, 130
Elmadjian, Fred, 104, 131,
EMDR (Eye Movement Desensitization and Reintegration), 152

Freud, Sigmund, 26, 125, 141–142, 146, 159, 168
Fromm-Reichmann, Frieda, 80–82, 86, 113, 122, 176

Goldstein, Kurt, 85–86

Haloperidol, 8, 84, 113
Hebephrenia, 91
Hoagland, Hudson, 5–22, 62, 106, 130–135
Huntington's disease, 7, 9, 51, 84, 167
Hydrotherapy, 73, 75–77

I Never Promised You a Rose Garden, 75, 80, 82
Insulin (shock or coma therapy), 22–24, 40, 91, 95, 130, 134, 142
Interpersonal Psychotherapy, 127–128, 152

Kline, Nathan, 139–140

Lithium, 172–173, 175, 184
Lobotomy, 31–32
Lysergic acid diethylamide #20 (LSD-25), 37, 82, 170–171

MacLean, Paul, 61–64
Madness in the Streets, 162, 177, 189–190
Manic (mania), 7, 39, 75–77, 94, 116, 123, 132–133, 145–157, 164, 172–174, 184, 187
Marijuana, 53, 150, 163, 180
McCulloch, Warren, 143–145

Nash, John, 24, 36, 179

Paraldehyde, 55
Paranoid (paranoia), 34, 37, 40, 47–49, 60, 81, 91, 99, 106, 123, 133, 171, 179
Parkinson's disease, 8, 9, 50,
Philips Scale, the, 132–133
PTSD (post traumatic stress disorder), 44, 152
Psychoanalysis, 69, 114, 115, 125, 132, 142, 143, 151, 153, 171, 184

Quietapine, 8, 180

Restraints, 5, 24, 55, 73, 76, 147, 168
Rosen, John, 121–124

Schizophrenia Project, 97, 108, 129–136, 130–133,
Schizophrenia (schizophrenic), 14–16, 22, 34, 36–39, 40–41, 48, 60, 75, 82, 83–84, 89–90, 91, 93–94, 98–99, 103–107, 109–110, 113, 122–124, 130, 140, 146, 158–159, 162–164, 171–175, 179
Scopolamine, 9, 55, 76
Sedatives, 6, 9, 39, 44–46, 50–52, 149
Syphilis, 7, 18, 39, 54, 73–75, 104, 167, 176

Torrey, E. Fuller, 177–178, 186
Treatment Advocacy Center, 187, 189–190
Truth Serum, 44–46

Wilson's disease, 7, 9, 50–51,
Worcester Biological Foundation, 6, 10, 17–18, 125–140, 170
Wortis, Joe, 22, 141–143

Zilboorg, Gregory, 121–124

About the Author

ENOCH CALLAWAY, M.D., who earned his medical degree at Columbia College of Physicians and Surgeons, is an Emeritus Professor of Psychiatry at the University of California, San Francisco, and former Director of Research at its Langley Porter Psychiatric Institute. His published works include over 100 papers, three edited volumes, and a monograph. He is a Distinguished Life Fellow of the American Psychiatric Association, past-president of the Society of Biological Psychiatry and the Society for Psychophysiological Research, and past board member for the American College of Neuropsychopharmacology. He has been editor of Archives of General Psychiatry, Biological Psychiatry, and Psychophysiology. Currently he serves on two Institutional Revue Boards, the board of a publicly held drug company, and sees patients part-time. Callaway lives in Tiburon, California